THE WAR WITHIN THE WAR

Sexual Violence Against Women and Girls in Eastern Congo

Human Rights Watch
New York • Washington • London • Brussels

ISBN: 1-56432-276-9
Library of Congress Control Number: 2002107517

Cover Photo: A woman in North Kivu who was assaulted by RCD soldiers in early 2002 and narrowly escaped rape.
© 2002 Juliane Kippenberg/Human Rights Watch

Cover design by Rafael Jiménez

Addresses for Human Rights Watch
350 Fifth Avenue, 34th Floor, New York, NY 10118-3299
Tel: (212) 290-4700, Fax: (212) 736-1300, E-mail: hrwnyc@hrw.org

1630 Connecticut Avenue, N.W., Suite 500, Washington, DC 20009
Tel: (202) 612-4321, Fax: (202) 612-4333, E-mail: hrwdc@hrw.org

33 Islington High Street, N1 9LH London, UK
Tel: (171) 713-1995, Fax: (171) 713-1800, E-mail: hrwatchuk@gn.apc.org

15 Rue Van Campenhout, 1000 Brussels, Belgium
Tel: (2) 732-2009, Fax: (2) 732-0471, E-mail: hrwatcheu@skynet.be

Web Site Address: http://www.hrw.org

Listserv address: To subscribe to the Human Rights Watch news e-mail list, send a blank e-mail message to subscribe@igc.topica.com.

Human Rights Watch is dedicated to
protecting the human rights of people around the world.

We stand with victims and activists to prevent
discrimination, to uphold political freedom, to protect people from
inhumane conduct in wartime, and to bring offenders to justice.

We investigate and expose
human rights violations and hold abusers accountable.

We challenge governments and those who hold power to end abusive
practices and respect international human rights law.

We enlist the public and the international
community to support the cause of human rights for all.

HUMAN RIGHTS WATCH

Human Rights Watch conducts regular, systematic investigations of human rights abuses in some seventy countries around the world. Our reputation for timely, reliable disclosures has made us an essential source of information for those concerned with human rights. We address the human rights practices of governments of all political stripes, of all geopolitical alignments, and of all ethnic and religious persuasions. Human Rights Watch defends freedom of thought and expression, due process and equal protection of the law, and a vigorous civil society; we document and denounce murders, disappearances, torture, arbitrary imprisonment, discrimination, and other abuses of internationally recognized human rights. Our goal is to hold governments accountable if they transgress the rights of their people.

Human Rights Watch began in 1978 with the founding of its Europe and Central Asia division (then known as Helsinki Watch). Today, it also includes divisions covering Africa, the Americas, Asia, and the Middle East. In addition, it includes three thematic divisions on arms, children's rights, and women's rights. It maintains offices in New York, Washington, Los Angeles, London, Brussels, Moscow, Tashkent, Tblisi, and Bangkok. Human Rights Watch is an independent, nongovernmental organization, supported by contributions from private individuals and foundations worldwide. It accepts no government funds, directly or indirectly.

The staff includes Kenneth Roth, executive director; Michele Alexander, development director; Reed Brody, advocacy director; Carroll Bogert, communications director; John T. Green, operations director, Barbara Guglielmo, finance director; Lotte Leicht, Brussels office director; Michael McClintock, deputy program director; Patrick Minges, publications director; Maria Pignataro Nielsen, human resources director; Malcolm Smart, program director; Wilder Tayler, legal and policy director; and Joanna Weschler, United Nations representative. Jonathan Fanton is the chair of the board. Robert L. Bernstein is the founding chair.

The regional directors of Human Rights Watch are Peter Takirambudde, Africa; José Miguel Vivanco, Americas; Sidney Jones, Asia; Elizabeth Andersen, Europe and Central Asia; and Hanny Megally, Middle East and North Africa. The thematic division directors are Joost R. Hiltermann, arms; Lois Whitman, children's; and LaShawn R. Jefferson, women's.

The members of the board of directors are Jonathan Fanton, Chair; Robert L. Bernstein, Founding Chair, Lisa Anderson, David M. Brown, William Carmichael, Dorothy Cullman, Gina Despres, Irene Diamond, Fiona Druckenmiller, Edith Everett, Michael Gellert, Vartan Gregorian, Alice H. Henkin, James F. Hoge, Jr., Stephen L. Kass, Marina Pinto Kaufman, Wendy Keys, Bruce J. Klatsky, Joanne Leedom - Ackerman, Josh Mailman, Joel Motley, Samuel K. Murumba, Jane Olson, Peter Osnos, Kathleen Peratis, Catherine Powell, Bruce Rabb, Sigrid Rausing, Orville Schell, Sid Sheinberg, Gary G. Sick, Malcolm Smith, Domna Stanton, John Studzinski, Maureen White, Maya Wiley. Emeritus Board: Roland Algrant, Adrian DeWind, and Malcolm Smith.

"My body has become sad. I have no happiness."
(thirty-five-year-old year old woman, raped by soldiers)

"There is a real madness with all this violence. This is a whole war within the war— another kind of attack on the Congolese people."
(counselor in eastern Congo)

ACKNOWLEDGEMENTS

Information presented in this report was gathered by a team composed of Human Rights Watch researchers and members of Congolese human rights associations based in Goma, Bukavu, and Uvira. We wish to thank our colleagues in eastern Congo, who risk their lives to defend the rights of others, for their commitment and assistance. We also wish to thank all those who took the time and courage to speak to the delegation, in particular the survivors themselves.

This report was written by Joanne Csete, director of Human Rights Watch's Program on HIV/AIDS and Human Rights, Juliane Kippenberg, NGO Liaison in the Africa Division of Human Rights Watch, and a consultant of the Africa division. Tony Tate, consultant, also contributed to the research. The report was reviewed by LaShawn R. Jefferson of the Women's Rights Division, Wilder Tayler, Legal and Policy Director, and Janet Fleischman and Suliman Baldo of the Africa Division of Human Rights Watch. It was edited by Alison Des Forges and Michael McClintock. Production and coordination assistance was provided by Jeff Scott, Patrick Minges, Maria Burnett-Gaudiani, and Veronica Mathushaj.

TABLE OF CONTENTS

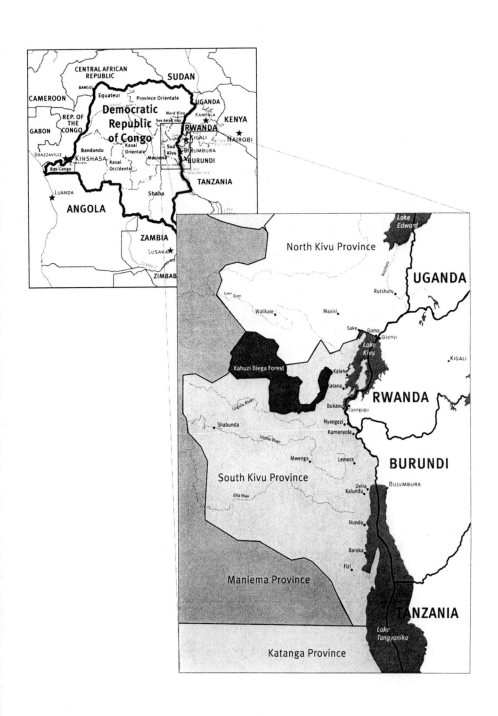

SUMMARY

Within the larger war in the eastern Democratic Republic of Congo (Congo) the warring parties carry out another war: that of sexual violence against women and girls. As military activities increase in one area after another, so do rapes and other crimes against women and girls. This report is based on research carried out in North and South Kivu provinces, an area controlled since 1998 by rebel forces fighting the government of President Kabila, the Rassemblement congolais pour la démocratie (RCD) and their patron, the Rwandan army. The Rwandan army, which occupies large parts of eastern Congo, and the RCD are opposed by several armed groups operating in eastern Congo, including Burundian armed groups and rebel Rwandans associated with the forces involved in the Rwandan genocide of 1994.

Sexual violence has been used as a weapon of war by most of the forces involved in this conflict. Combatants of the RCD, Rwandan soldiers, as well as combatants of the forces opposed to them— Mai-Mai, armed groups of Rwandan Hutu, and Burundian rebels of the Forces for the Defense of Democracy (Forces pour la défense de la démocratie, FDD) and Front for National Liberation (Front pour la libération nationale, FNL) - frequently and sometimes systematically raped women and girls in the last year.

In some cases soldiers and combatants raped women and girls as part of a more general attack in which they killed and injured civilians and pillaged and destroyed their property. They did this to terrorize communities into accepting their control or to punish them for real or supposed aid to opposing forces, particularly if they themselves had recently been attacked by these forces. In cases where there was no larger attack, individuals or small groups of soldiers and combatants also raped women and girls whom they found in the fields, in the forest, along the roads, or in their homes.

The war which has ravaged this region intermittently since 1996 has destroyed the local economy. Driven by desperate poverty, women who provided the resources to keep their families alive continued going to the fields to cultivate, to the forest to make charcoal, or to markets to trade their goods even though doing so put them at risk of sexual violence. Soldiers and combatants preyed upon such women and girls as well as on others who had fled combat to live in temporary and fragile structures in the forest. In many cases, combatants abducted women and girls and took them to their bases in the forest where they forced them to provide sexual services and domestic labor, sometimes for periods of more than a year. Among the hundreds of thousands displaced by the war were many women who sought safety for themselves and their families in towns. Instead of finding security, some were raped by soldiers from nearby military camps or by government officials.

1

Some rapists aggravated their crimes by other acts of extraordinary brutality, shooting victims in the vagina or mutilating them with knives or razor blades. Some attacked girls as young as five years of age or elderly women as old as eighty. Some killed their victims outright while others left them to die of their injuries.

This report focuses on crimes of sexual violence committed by soldiers and other combatants. But rape and other sexual crimes are not just carried out by armed factions but also increasingly by police and others in positions of authority and power, and by opportunistic common criminals and bandits, taking advantage of the prevailing climate of impunity and the culture of violence against women and girls. While crimes committed by common criminals are not examined in detail in this report, it does document cases of attacks by armed men when there are indications that the perpetrators might have been combatants. Such indications can be the language of the attackers, their weapons, their degree of organization or the pattern of abuse against civilians.

Irregular combatants and regular soldiers responsible for acts of sexual violence commit war crimes. In some cases their crimes could amount to crimes against humanity. The RCD, widely described as a proxy of the Rwandan government, administers large parts of eastern Congo, including North and South Kivu provinces, though this control is mostly limited to the cities and towns. Some courts do function and have punished cases of rape by private citizens. Yet soldiers and other combatants commit crimes of sexual violence with virtually total impunity, and neither police nor judicial authorities pursue rape cases seriously. Few women brought charges against rapists, in part because they knew there was little chance of seeing the criminal condemned, in part because they feared the social stigma attached to being known as a rape victim.

The fear of being stigmatized also kept some victims from seeking medical attention. Many others who wished medical help had nowhere to go. Medical services, eroded over decades of misrule, collapsed completely in many communities during the war. The lack of such assistance was particularly critical given the prevalence of human immunodeficiency virus (HIV) among soldiers and irregular combatants, estimated by one expert at 60 percent among military forces in the region. With the increase in rapes, many women were exposed not just to acquired immune deficiency syndrome (AIDS) but also to other sexually transmitted diseases (STDs). They, like many of those seriously injured by rape and other sexually assaults, have not been able to receive appropriate medical treatment.

These crimes of sexual violence have direct, profound, and life-changing consequences for the women and girls attacked and for their wider communities.

Many women and girls will never recover from the physical, psychological, and social effects of these assaults and some will die from them. A significant number became pregnant as a result of rape and now struggle to provide for the children they have borne. Some women and girls have been rejected by their husbands and families and ostracized by the wider community because they were raped or because they are thought to be infected with HIV/AIDS. Survivors of rape and other forms of sexual violence must now attempt to make a new life for themselves, sometimes by relocating to communities far from their former homes. A thirty-five year old woman was raped by Rwandan soldiers in August 1998, and her husband killed by the same attackers. Later she was chased away by her husband's family. She told Human Rights Watch: "My body has become sad. I have no happiness."

Brutality against civilians, and specifically sexual violence, is an integral part of the war in eastern Congo. Forces involved in acts of sexual violence against women and girls continue to be rewarded by their leadership and by their powerful patrons for their actions. As long as the climate of impunity persists in eastern Congo, women and girls will continue to be targeted in the war within a war.

RECOMMENDATIONS

To the Government of Rwanda and the Rassemblement Congolais pour la Démocratie (RCD)

- Issue clear instructions to all troops under RCD and government of Rwanda control to immediately cease all sexual violence against women and girls as well as all other violations of international humanitarian law.

- Establish a full investigation into acts of sexual violence committed by Rwandan Patriotic Army and RCD forces. The findings of such investigations should be made public. Take appropriate measures to protect the safety, physical and psychological well-being, dignity, and privacy of victims and witnesses who bring complaints of sexual violence. Those allegedly responsible for acts of sexual violence, including those in positions of command responsibility who may have ordered or acquiesced in these violations of international humanitarian law, must be tried in proceedings that conform to international standards of due process and removed from office pending trial. The victims of sexual violence should be compensated.

- Allow civil society to operate freely, to speak out critically, and to carry out investigations into crimes of sexual violence. Extend invitations to the relevant United Nations rapporteurs as well as international organizations and journalists to carry out investigations into sexual violence against women and girls, ensuring that the privacy and security of victims and witnesses will be assured.

- Facilitate local and international programs of humanitarian assistance for victims of sexual violence and to other civilian populations in need of assistance.

- Provide training to Rwandan Patriotic Army and RCD troops on the rights of women and girls and on national and international law barring sexual violence.

- Provide troops and public officials with training and counseling on sexually transmitted diseases, including HIV/AIDS; provide confidential HIV testing and counseling and free or subsidized condoms.

To the Mai-Mai and predominantly Hutu armed groups operating in eastern Congo

- Issue clear instructions to all combatants under the control of Mai-Mai or predominantly Hutu armed groups to immediately cease all sexual violence against women and girls, as well as all other violations of international humanitarian law.

- Allow full access for nongovernmental organizations, both national and international, medical professionals and humanitarian agencies providing information and services to victims of sexual violence or investigating these acts.

To the Government of the Democratic Republic of Congo

- Stop providing any financial or military assistance to armed groups in eastern Congo whose members have committed serious human rights abuses, including Mai-Mai or predominantly Hutu armed groups.

- Use your influence to pressure armed groups in eastern Congo, in particular, Mai-Mai or predominantly Hutu armed groups, to immediately cease all acts of sexual violence against women and girls.

- Facilitate investigations into human rights abuses, particularly sexual violence in the eastern Congo, by the United Nations special rapporteur on violence against women and the United Nations special rapporteur on the situation of human rights in the Democratic Republic of Congo

To the United Nations

- Expand the mandate and capacity of the United Nations Observer Mission in the Congo (MONUC) to include protecting civilians against violations of international humanitarian law, including particularly the protection of women and girls. Ensure that civilian components of MONUC, particularly child protection officers, human rights observers, and humanitarian officers, are tasked directly with monitoring and reporting on sexual violence.

- Reinforce training of MONUC soldiers and staff on sexual violence and on HIV/AIDS, as specified by the U.N. General Assembly Declaration of Commitment at the special session on HIV/AIDS. Ensure availability of confidential HIV testing and counseling as well as condoms for soldiers and staff. Immediately investigate any credible allegations of crimes of sexual violence committed by MONUC troops; publish the results of such investigations, including the charges now reportedly pending against a Moroccan soldier. Ensure that those responsible are brought to justice by their national military justice systems and that all pertinent information gathered by the U.N. is provided to those authorities.

- Address the question of impunity for atrocities in Congo, and in particular, establish a U.N. Commission of Experts to investigate and determine responsibility for grave violations of human rights and humanitarian law in Congo, including sexual violence. The Commission of Experts should recommend to the Security Council an appropriate mechanism to bring to justice persons responsible for such violations.

- Increase the human and financial resources of the field office of the U.N. High Commissioner for Human Rights in Congo (HRFOC) to enable it to better monitor and report crimes of sexual violence and to better assist national nongovernmental organizations working on such issues. Employ staff with special expertise on women's rights. Establish HRFOC field offices in crisis areas such as Uvira or ensure regular visits to this area by staff from HRFOC field offices.

- Direct the staff of U.N. agencies working in eastern Congo to give priority to programs focused on the rights of women and girls, the elimination of sexual violence, and the prevention and treatment of HIV/AIDS and other sexually transmitted diseases.

- Ensure that the Global Fund To Fight AIDS, Tuberculosis and Malaria makes the combat against HIV/AIDS in Congo a priority.

To Donor Governments

- Strongly denounce crimes of sexual violence, as well as other violations of human rights and humanitarian law by all parties and insist on accountability for the perpetrators. Apply strong and constant pressure on all governments and non-state actors involved in the conflict to observe their obligations under human rights and humanitarian law.

- Provide greatly increased financial, technical, and political support for monitoring and documenting sexual violence and for protecting victims and providing them with medical, legal, and social support services. Where possible channel such assistance through nongovernmental organizations, including local women's and human rights organizations. Support all credible efforts by legal or defacto authorities to bring perpetrators of sexual violence to justice, including the protection of witnesses.

- Encourage the Security Council to create a U.N. Commission of Experts to investigate and determine responsibility for grave violations of human rights and humanitarian law in Congo and recommend an appropriate mechanism to bring to justice perpetrators.

- Assist the development and maintenance of programs and services related to HIV/AIDS and other sexually transmitted diseases. These should provide information on HIV prevention and AIDS care, especially for young people and women; HIV testing and counseling services; information on the prevention of mother-to-child transmission; free condoms; treatment for opportunistic infections; and long-term treatment with antiretroviral drugs as they become more affordable.

- Scrutinize all economic assistance to states involved in the conflict in Congo to ensure that funds earmarked for social and economic development programs do not end up financing abusive conduct by any party to the conflict.

- The Multi-Donor Trust Fund of the World Bank should add an explicit focus on issues affecting women and girls in eastern Congo, including providing resources for programs to protect women from sexual crimes, such as training, education and other social support services to women impacted by the crisis, and support for local nongovernmental organizations to assist women in the region.

METHODOLOGY

This report is based on a three-week mission by Human Rights Watch researchers to the Democratic Republic of Congo (Congo) and Rwanda in October and November 2001 and on prior and subsequent research. Our team carried out research in Bukavu, Shabunda, and Uvira in South Kivu province and in and around Goma in North Kivu province together with colleagues from the Congolese human rights organizations Héritiers de la Justice, Réseau des Femmes pour la Défense des Droits et la Paix, Promotion et Appui aux Initiatives Féminines, Solidarité pour la Promotion Sociale et la Paix, Action Sociale pour la Paix et le Développement and several associations in Uvira.[1] We interviewed more than fifty women and girls[2] who had been subjected to sexual or gender-based violence[3] as well as others who had escaped an attempted rape. We also spoke with relatives of women and girls who had either been raped or escaped rape and with others who had witnessed assaults. Those interviewed came from both towns and rural areas. In addition, we interviewed local authorities, religious and health personnel, and representatives of local and international nongovernmental organizations (NGOs) working in the areas of human rights, women's rights, and health, and United Nations (U.N.) officials. We participated in meetings with associations of rape victims, women's organizations, and support groups for women infected with HIV or suffering from AIDS.

Research into sexual violence is highly sensitive and requires taking into account the consequences for the survivors/victims[4] of speaking out— whether in terms of their immediate security, their standing in the community, or their

---

[1] Human rights colleagues from Uvira have asked that their associations not be named in this report.

[2] In this report the terms "girls" and "boys" refer to children. Article 219 of the Congolese Family Code defines a child as a person under the age of eighteen. Under international law, persons below the age of eighteen are considered children (art. 1 of the Convention on the Rights of the Child, September 2, 1990). All states are party to the Convention on the Rights of the Child except for the United States of America and Somalia.

[3] The term "sexual violence" is used in this report to refer to all forms of violence of a sexual nature, such as rape, attempted rape, sexual assault, and sexual threat. Gender-based violence is violence directed at an individual, male or female, based on his or her specific gender role in society, such as, in the case of women and girls, being forced to cook and clean. Sexual and gender-based violence are frequently associated.

[4] Women and girls who have been raped can be presented and/or perceived either as victims or survivors and there is an ongoing debate as to which is the more appropriate term. In this report both terms are used interchangeably without significant distinction.

8

psychological and emotional states.[5] Many victims are threatened with further harm by the perpetrators if they speak of the rape and they are reluctant to report the crime. Some risk their lives by revealing what happened to them. If the perpetrators are part of the military or are linked to civilian authorities in control of the immediate area, the risk of talking publicly of the rape may increase. Members of nongovernmental organizations and medical and religious personnel who have discussed rapes, particularly if their comments imply criticism of local authorities, have also been threatened with harm and some of them subsequently hesitate to talk about the problem. Rape victims are often stigmatized by the rest of the community and even by their own family members. Speaking about the crime may expose survivors to such rejection. Family members may share the concerns of the survivors about security and standing in the community and may urge them to keep silence. Victims who recount the circumstances of the crime, moreover, may suffer from renewed or intensified psychological and physical stress reactions that characterize post traumatic stress syndrome.

Taking into consideration these concerns, we interviewed victims in the presence only of a translator, if needed, and a family member or friend, health professional or religious counselor, if the presence of such a person was desired by the interviewee. In almost all cases the translator was a person known to the interviewee. Ordinarily all present were women. In the few cases where a man was present, it was with the permission of the interviewee. In order to guarantee the confidentiality of all information, the names of interviewees have been changed and sometimes details of dates and locations of interviews have been omitted in this report. While we sought as much information as possible from each interview, the well-being of the interviewee was always paramount and some interviews were cut short as a result.

We were struck by the courage and strength of many survivors who shared their experiences with us despite the risks, fear, and embarrassment that this entailed. A twelve-year-old girl who was raped concluded her testimony by saying she was willing to talk about the rape because "it is important that this doesn't happen to other people."[6]

---

[5] On the methodological issues, see Agnès Callamard, *A Methodology for Gender-Sensitive Research* (Quebec: Amnesty International Publications and the International Centre for Human Rights and Democratic Development, 1999); *Documenting Human Rights Violations by State Agents: Sexual Violence* (Quebec: Amnesty International Publications and the International Centre for Human Rights and Democratic Development, 1999).

[6] Human Rights Watch interview, Goma, October 25, 2001.

This report is part of a larger project by Human Rights Watch and Congolese human rights associations to combat human rights violations, in particular sexual violence, in Congo. In September 2000, Human Rights Watch and Héritiers de la Justice organized a workshop with women's and human rights associations from Bukavu on this issue. In October 2001, Human Rights Watch and Promotion et Appui aux Initiatives Feminines (PAIF) led a second workshop for members of human rights and women's organizations, medical personnel, and lawyers from North and South Kivu to examine the medical and human rights aspects of sexual violence in the context of the war in Congo.

CONTEXT

Background to the Conflict

The war which has spurred an increase in crimes of sexual violence against women in the eastern Congo is the local manifestation of a complex regional conflict which began in 1996 and has involved seven nations and many groups of armed combatants.

In 1994 the Rwandan government, dominant parts of its army (Forces Armées Rwandaises, FAR), and members of the Interahamwe[7] militia directed a genocide against the Tutsi of Rwanda which took more than half a million lives. After being defeated by the Rwandan Patriotic Army (RPA), the military force of the Rwandan Patriotic Front (RPF), the government responsible for the genocide then led more than a million Hutu into exile in Congo, then Zaire, where civilian refugees and the military together established themselves in camps along the border. Under the direction of the defeated political and military leaders, soldiers and militia reorganized and rearmed within the refugee population, preparing for new attacks on Rwanda. Although such military activity was prohibited by international convention, neither U.N. agencies nor the larger international community intervened to halt the preparations.[8]

In late 1996 the Rwandan government sent its troops into the Congo, asserting the need to impede preparations for attacks on Rwanda as well as any obligation to protect the Banyamulenge, Congolese of the Tutsi ethnic group, who were being threatened by local and national Congolese political authorities. The Rwandan soldiers together with combatants of the Allied Democratic Forces for the Liberation of Congo (Alliance des Forces Démocratiques pour la Libération du Congo-Zaire, AFDL), a hastily organized coalition of Congolese forces, attacked the camps and killed tens of thousands of Rwandans, many of them unarmed civilian refugees. Hundreds of thousands of refugees then returned to Rwanda, some of them voluntarily, some of them forced to do so by Rwandan government troops. Some two hundred thousand Rwandans fled westward through the forests. Many of the civilians were massacred in the

---

[7] The Interahamwe (meaning literally "those who stand or attack together" in Kinyarwanda) officially referred to the youth wing of the former ruling party, the Mouvement Republicain Nationale Démocratique (MRND), but it came to describe all militia participating in the genocide regardless of party affiliation. See Human Rights Watch/ Fédération Internationale des Ligues des Droits de l'Homme, *Leave None to Tell the Story: Genocide in Rwanda* (New York: Human Rights Watch/ Fédération Internationale des Ligues des Droits de l'Homme, 1999), and see Human Rights Watch, *Shattered Lives. Sexual Violence during the Rwandan Genocide and its Aftermath* (New York: Human Rights Watch, 1996).

[8] Human Rights Watch, "Rearming with Impunity," *A Human Rights Watch Report*, vol. 7, no. 4 , May 1995.

following months by RPA or AFDL troops but several thousand ex-FAR and militia members regrouped to resume fighting the Rwandan government forces in Congo and later in Rwanda.[9]

Uganda, too, sent troops to support the AFDL. Under the leadership of Laurent Kabila, the rebel force and its Rwandan and Ugandan allies marched on the Congolese capital, Kinshasa, and in May 1997 overthrew President Mobutu. Fourteen months later Laurent Kabila and his government sought to oust their foreign backers and Rwanda and Uganda then offered their support to a new rebellion against the Congolese government led by the RCD. To combat this alliance, President Kabila enlisted assistance, including troops and military aircraft from Zimbabwe, Angola, and Namibia.

This report deals only with territory under the control of Rwanda and RCD-Goma: RCD is used in this report to refer only to RCD-Goma although the RCD has undergone several divisions since its formation in 1998. RCD-Goma refers to the group based in Goma which controls most of North and South Kivu, parts of Maniema, Orientale, and Katanga, and a large part of Kasai Orientale provinces. RCD-Goma is widely described as proxy of the Rwandan government and dominated by forces of the Rwandan army which occupies this territory. The RCD-Goma is separate from both RCD-Kisangani and RCD-ML (RCD-Liberation Movement).

In July 1999 the main foreign contenders signed a cease-fire accord at Lusaka. But it was only in February 2001, after the assassination of Laurent Kabila and the installation of his son Joseph Kabila as president, that Ugandan and Rwandan troops and other foreign forces partially disengaged along the battlefront. [10] A United Nations peacekeeping force, the U.N. Observation

---

[9] See Human Rights Watch, "What Kabila is Hiding, Civilian Killings and Impunity in Congo," *A Human Rights Watch Report*, vol. 9, no. 5(A), October, 1997 and Human Rights Watch, "Uncertain Course: Transition and Human Rights Violations in the Congo," *A Human Rights Watch Report*, vol. 9, no. 9(A), December, 1997 (both also available in French and available on the Human Rights Watch web site: http://www.hrw.org). To date no action has been taken to bring those who massacred the refugees to justice. The U.N. has made two efforts to document these war crimes but has failed to complete their work. After a team of experts appointed by the Secretary-General delivered a report on June 30, 1998 to the Security Council implicating Congolese and Rwandan soldiers in crimes against humanity against and possible genocide of displaced Rwandans, the U.N. Security Council charged the Congolese and Rwandan governments with carrying forward the investigation (see Presidential Statement dated July 13, 1998 S/PRST/1998/20). Neither has done so.

[10] The signatories to the agreement included the Congolese government and its allies, Zimbabwe, Angola and Namibia; the RCD and its patron, Rwanda; and the Movement for the Liberation of Congo (Mouvement pour la Libération du Congo, MLC) and its patron, Uganda.

Mission in the Congo (MONUC), was put in place to supervise the ceasefire and the demobilization of combatants. Namibia withdrew its troops and Uganda brought home some of its soldiers, although it later sent some troops back into the Congo. Zimbabwe, Burundi, and Rwanda said their troops would also be withdrawn, but fixed no date for this action.[11] In October and November 2001 the Rwandan command shifted some of its troops to new posts in the eastern Congo.[12]

In the second half of 2001, there was little military activity on the front lines but combat continued in the Kivus, characterized by systematic and grave violations of international humanitarian law by all parties.[13]

The Lusaka agreement provides for an Inter-Congolese Dialogue to bring together representatives from the Congolese government, the rebel forces opposed to it, the unarmed political opposition, and civil society. After numerous postponements, the talks began in mid-October 2001 but quickly collapsed; they are finally took place in Sun City, South Africa, in early 2002. They led to a partial power-sharing agreement between the government of the Democratic Republic of Congo, the rebel MLC and most members of the unarmed opposition and civil society groups, but excluded the RCD and failed to secure peace with Rwanda.[14]

---

[11] Ninth report of the Secretary-General on the UN Organization Mission in DR Congo, S/2001/970, Paragraph 30.

[12] Human Rights Watch interviews, Bukavu and Uvira, October/ November 2001; this movement of RPA troops continued as recently as January 2002, according to a witness in Bukavu, Human Rights Watch telephone interview, January 8, 2002.

[13] See, for example, "Casualties of War: Civilians, Rule of Law, and Democratic Freedoms," *A Human Rights Watch Report*, vol. 11, no. 1(A), February 1999; "Eastern Congo Ravaged: Killing Civilians and Silencing Protest," *A Human Rights Watch Report*, vol.12, no 3 (A), May 2000; "Uganda in Eastern DRC: Fueling political and ethnic strife," *A Human Rights Watch Report*, vol. 13, No. 2(A), March 2001; and "Reluctant Recruits: Children and Adults Forcibly Recruited for Military Service in North Kivu," *A Human Rights Watch Report*, vol. 13, No. 3(A), May 2001 (all also available in French and available on the Human Rights Watch web site: http://www.hrw.org).

[14] See "The Inter-Congolese Dialogue: Political Negotiation or Game of Bluff?" International Crisis Group, November 16, 2001, located at http://www.crisisweb.org/projects/showreport.cfm?reportid=488, and "Storm Clouds over Sun City: The Urgent Need to Recast the Congolese Peace Process", International Crisis Group, May 14, 2002, located at http://www.crisisweb.org/projects/showreport.cfm?reportid=652 (accessed May 23,2002).

The Situation in the Kivus

RCD, RPA, and the Burundian Army

The RCD claims to control a significant part of eastern Congo, including most of the provinces of North and South Kivu. It says it administers this area in accord with Congolese law and it has appointed governors and other administrative officials. But, in some areas, such as Shabunda territory, various local armed groups control most of the countryside and keep the RCD confined to the towns.

The Rwandan government, one of the original backers of the RCD and now its most important supporter, exercises considerable influence over its decisions. Rwanda has stationed thousands of troops in the Kivus and elsewhere in eastern Congo, claiming they are there to combat ex-FAR, Interahamwe, and others opposed to it. Rwanda draws enormous profit from the illegal exploitation of Congolese resources, providing another and perhaps more important motive for its determination to keep its forces on Congolese soil. A panel of experts appointed by the U.N. Security Council established in mid-2001 that Rwanda is growing rich at the expense of the Congo.[15]

In the southern part of South Kivu, the Burundian army also assists the RCD, though less extensively than does the RPA. Its soldiers are fighting along Lake Tanganyika against the Burundian rebel groups FDD and FNL which have bases on Congolese territory and which oppose the RCD. The Burundian government does not exert any significant political influence on the RCD nor has it engaged in significant exploitation of Congolese resources.

The Rwandan Patriotic Army originally was predominantly Tutsi; the number of Hutu in its ranks has increased considerably in recent years, but most high-ranking officers remain Tutsi. Similarly, Congolese of the Tutsi ethnic group – called Banyamulenge – play a major role in the RCD and Tutsi constitute the majority of officers of the Burundian forces. Congolese who are not Tutsi, particularly those opposed to the presence of Rwandan and Burundian government forces on their soil, often refer to members of any of these forces as "Tutsi," usually with negative connotations. In this report, we avoid such use unless directly quoting witnesses.

---

[15] See U.N. Security Council, "Interim Report of the UN Expert Panel Report on the Illegal Exploitation of Natural Resources and Other Forms of Wealth of DR Congo," S/2000/49, 20th December 2000; See also "Scramble for the Congo: Anatomy of an Ugly War," International Crisis Group Africa Report No. 26, 20th December 2000 (http://www.crisisweb.org/projects/showreport.cfm?reportid=130, accessed May 22, 2002).

Predominantly Hutu Armed Groups and "Interahamwe"

A number of armed groups made up primarily of Rwandan Hutu are fighting against the RCD, the RPA, and the Burundian army in the Kivus. Some of these combatants, particularly those in positions of command, participated in the Rwandan genocide, but many others—probably the majority—did not. Many persons, both Congolese and foreign, refer to these combatants globally as Interahamwe, a practice which wrongly attributes genocidal guilt to all. Some Congolese, whether Hutu or not, have also joined these groups. In the remainder of this report, we avoid the term Interahamwe unless directly quoting witnesses.[16]

The main military force of Rwandan Hutu in eastern Congo is the Army for the Liberation of Rwanda (Armée pour la liberation du Rwanda, ALIR) which operates in North Kivu as ALIR I and in South Kivu as ALIR II. Other Rwandan Hutu combatants participate in the Democratic Forces for the Liberation of Rwanda (Forces démocratiques pour la liberation du Rwanda, FDLR), a group affiliated more closely with the Congolese army (Forces Armées Congolaises, FAC) and operating mostly in South Kivu and Katanga.[17] Of an estimated 10,000 to 15,000 Rwandan Hutu rebels combatants in the Congo, perhaps half fight together with the FAC while the rest operate more or less autonomously in the Kivus in groups of varying size. Although ordinarily hostile to the RPA and RCD, some Hutu rebel groups are reported to have made short-term arrangements with them, particularly where necessary to facilitate exploitation of local mineral resources.

The FDD, a Burundian Hutu rebel group, has a strong presence in eastern Congo, mostly in South Kivu and Katanga provinces. Until recently they have been headquartered in Lubumbashi, from where its forces operated in conjunction with the FAC. It and the smaller FNL carry out military activities in South Kivu and from there across the border into Burundi.

Under Laurent Kabila, the Congolese government and army provided logistical and military support to rebel Rwandan Hutu and Burundian armed

---

[16] It has been estimated that as many as 15,000 "Rwandan Hutu armed forces" are in Congo, with approximately half fighting alongside government troops and half "operating as militias in the Kivus in eastern Congo (in Masisi, Shabunda, Kahuzi-Biega, and Virunga areas)." International Crisis Group, "Disarmament in the Congo: Investing in Conflict Prevention," Africa Briefing, June 12, 2001, p. 2.

[17] On these forces, in particular ALIR, see "Rwanda: Observing the Rules of War?" *A Human Rights Watch Report,* vol.13, No.8 (A), December 2001.

groups. When Joseph Kabila took power in early 2001, he promised to end this support, but reports in mid 2001 indicated that he had not yet done so.[18]

In January 2002, the new Burundian government—a broad-based government installed in November 2001 as part of the Arusha Peace Agreement—announced the withdrawal of its forces from Congo. In return, the Congolese government promised to stop supporting the FDD, thus appearing to acknowledge that the support continued at least until that time. As of this writing, Burundian government troops remained in Congo.

Mai-Mai

The term Mai-Mai[19] originally applied to numerous locally based groups of combatants committed to the defense of their communities against outsiders, sometimes defined as Rwandan, Burundian, or Ugandan government soldiers, sometimes defined as Rwandan or Burundian rebel combatants, and sometimes defined as Congolese of other ethnic groups, particularly those who speak Kinyarwanda or are of Tutsi origin. For some Congolese the Mai-Mai represent "the popular resistance."[20] A Congolese priest told our research team, "We are all Mai-Mai—it's self-defense. We must show the Rwandans that they control nothing."[21] A doctor said, "The Mai-Mai are our colleagues. It's a popular revolution....They are the people of the village."[22]

During the course of the war, some Mai-Mai came to focus on increasing their own wealth and power in the name of defending their communities. They became opportunistic predators, killing, raping and pillaging local civilians. Some witnesses said this change resulted from intensified conflict with foreign troops over the control over local resources from which the Mai-Mai also intended to benefit.[23] One Congolese human rights activist commented, "There

---

[18] Human Rights Watch interview, Bujumbura, July 2001. See also the report by the International Crisis Group, "Disarmament in the Congo: Investing in Conflict Prevention," the Congo government continues to provide material support for these groups, p.4—5.

[19] Mai-Mai (also May-May or Mayi-Mayi) are sometimes known as the Popular Armed Forces (Forces Armées Populaire, or FAP). The name comes from the Kiswahili word "mayi" for water. Many Mai-Mai groups believe that they can be protected through rituals and charms which are said to transform bullets into water.

[20] Human Rights Watch interview, October 20, 2001.

[21] Human Rights Watch interview, October 19, 2001.

[22] Human Rights Watch interview, Bukavu, October 20, 2001.

[23] Human Rights Watch interview, Bukavu, October 20, 2001. See U.N. Security Council, "Interim Report of the UN Expert Panel Report on the Illegal Exploitation of

are true and false Mai-Mai. True Mai-Mai are the ones who would not rape—they can't touch women. They have rules."[24] Another activist explained, "When Kabila arrived with the Tutsi, bandits started invading the movement, taking advantage of opportunities presented by poverty and famine. [The Mai-Mai] became bandits because of a lack of structure."[25] A Congolese lawyer concurred, "Mai-Mai have a certain philosophy. Others have rallied to the Mai-Mai but don't follow their principles and that leads to indiscipline." A thirty-two-year-old woman who was raped by three Mai-Mai was asked how she knew the perpetrators were Mai-Mai. "People recognized them. Everyone is Mai-Mai. At the beginning [of the conflict] they were good, but they became bad."[26] Some Mai-Mai groups include Rwandan and Burundian Hutu.

Mai-Mai groups have no central command or uniform regulations. Some cooperate loosely with others, but many remain autonomous and sometimes even engage in combat with other Mai-Mai. Some Mai-Mai have allied with predominantly Hutu rebel groups, with the Congolese government, and even with Ugandan army forces and the RPA and RCD, often in short-term arrangements which can shift suddenly. The Congolese government reportedly tried to organize Mai-Mai forces under its control without success in-mid 2001. It is said to be continuing logistical and military support to some groups. [27]

Socio-economic Conditions, Displacement and Health Care
The war has taken an enormous toll on ordinary people, costing the lives of 2.5 of the 20 million civilians in eastern Congo between 1998 and 2001, according to an estimate done by the International Rescue Committee. These deaths, estimated to be the number beyond that which would normally be expected for this population during this period, are more due to lack of food, clean water, medicine and shelter than to combat itself.[28] Five years of war has

---

Natural Resources and Other Forms of Wealth of DR Congo," S/2000/49, 20th December 2000; see also "Scramble for the Congo: Anatomy of an Ugly War," International Crisis Group Africa Report No 26, 20th December 2000 (http://www.crisisweb.org/projects/showreport.cfm?reportid=130, accessed May 22, 2002).

[24] Human Rights Watch interview, Bukavu, October 20, 2001.

[25] Human Rights Watch interview, Bukavu, October 20, 2001.

[26] Human Rights Watch interview, Shabunda, October 22, 2001.

[27] Human Rights Watch interviews in Uvira, July 2001.

[28] International Rescue Committee, Mortality in Eastern Democratic Republic of Congo, Results from Eleven Mortality Surveys, 2001. The full report can be found on the IRC web site: www.theIRC.org/mortality.cfm, accessed May 22, 2002). The situation is

virtually eliminated what remained of Congo's infrastructure after thirty years of mismanagement and erosion under Mobutu—its health, judicial and educational services, its road and communication networks. State employees, including health and judicial personnel, are unpaid and demoralized, unemployment is widespread, corruption has become necessary for most to survive, and, despite the country's enormous mineral wealth, the economy has collapsed.[29] According to one study done in North Kivu, the majority of the people in that province lived on the equivalent of approximately U.S. $0.20 per day at the end of 2000.[30]

An estimated four-fifths of rural families have fled their homes at least once in the past five years.[31] Some 760,000 people are currently displaced in North Kivu and 225,000 more in South Kivu, accounting for almost half of the whole country's total of 2,045,000 internally displaced persons.[32] No longer within solid walls, sometimes living dispersed in the forest, displaced persons— particularly women and girls—had little protection if attacked by soldiers and combatants. Because farmers fled or were prevented from going to their fields or taking their produce to market, food production declined and malnutrition increased. According to aid workers who talked with Human Rights Watch researchers, malnutrition in one part of South Kivu was so serious in late 2001 that only adults were still able to walk to nutritional centers for assistance; children and the elderly lacked the strength to make the journey.[33]

---

so bad that IRC found that in some districts an estimated 75 percent of children have died or will die before their second birthday—children who have known nothing but war in their short lives.

[29] Congo is currently ranked 152nd on the UNDP Human Development Index of 174 countries. UN OCHA Great Lakes regional Office, "Affected Populations in the Great Lakes Region (as of 3 September 2001)," Nairobi, p. 12, posted on ReliefWeb.

[30] ASRAMES, Enquête socio-économique Nord-Kivu, Décembre 2000, quoted in *Report of the WHO/UNICEF Joint Mission, Democratic Republic of Congo, 18-19 June 2001*, Kinshasa, June 28, 2001.

[31] U.N. OCHA, "Chronicles of a Humanitarian Crisis, year 2000, Democratic Republic of Congo," quoted in Save the Children, Oxfam and Christian Aid, "No End In Sight, The human tragedy of the conflict in the Democratic Republic of Congo," August 2001, p.10.

[32] U.N. OCHA Great Lakes regional Office, "Affected Populations in the Great Lakes Region (as of 3 September 2001)," Nairobi, p. 11, posted on ReliefWeb (www.reliefweb.int). See map of affected populations in Congo by province, refugees and internally displaced, prepared by OCHA Great Lakes Regional Office, Nairobi, September 2001 on the same site.

[33] Human Rights Watch interview, Uvira, October 30, 2001.

Impoverished people rarely found the money needed to pay for health services. Even those with resources found the distance too great or the roads too insecure to go to a health center or clinic. In addition many health facilities no longer functioned because personnel had fled, because supplies were exhausted, or because the buildings had been damaged or destroyed. According to a report by the World Health Organization (WHO) and United Nations Children's Fund (UNICEF), more than 70 percent of the Congolese population is effectively without access to formal health care because they lack money for the services or because they cannot get to the facilities.[34] About 1,837 women per 100,000 die in childbirth in Congo, over three times the average of other African nations.[35]

All parties to the conflict have targeted hospitals and health clinics, sometimes to pillage equipment and supplies and sometimes to punish staff for having supposedly aided their opponents or to prevent them from rendering such aid in the future.[36] "We are between the hammer and the anvil," complained a nurse whose medical center had been attacked by RCD troops. The soldiers believed that the center had never been attacked by Hutu armed groups or Mai-Mai and that its staff must therefore be complicit with the rebels. In fact the soldiers were wrong. The center had been previously pillaged by one such group before it was attacked by the RCD forces.[37]

---

[34] *Report of the WHO/UNICEF Joint Mission, Democratic Republic of Congo, 18-19 June 2001*, Kinshasa, June 28, 2001; citing B. Criel Van der Stuft and W. VanLerberghe, "The Bwamanda Hospital Insurance Scheme: A study of its impact on hospital utilization patterns," *Social Science & Medicine* 48 (1999), pp. 897-911; B. Criel & W. Van Dormael, "Voluntary Health Insurance in Bwamanda, Democratic Republic of Congo, An exploration of its meanings to the community," *Tropical Medicine and International Health* 3,8 (1998), pp. 640-653; and World Health Organisation, "Evaluation des systemes de surveillance epidemiologique en RDC: Kinshasa, Province du Bas-Congo, du Kasai Occidental et du Katanga," April 2000. The WHO/UNICEF Joint Mission Report also states: "Right now in Congo, the vast majority of health and education services is a business in which struggling workers have to play off their family's survival against that of their patients and pupils...Rational treatment and prescribing are abandoned when giving fewer or more appropriate drugs can be detrimental to income."

[35] World Health Organization, "Democratic Republic of Congo Health Update," July 2001, p. 3.

[36] Human Rights Watch interview, Bukavu, October 20, 2001. For this reason, particular care is taken in this report not to identify doctors and nurses or the establishment they work in.

[37] Human Rights Watch interviews, October, 2001; and copy correspondence handed to Human Rights Watch detailing examples of these types of incidents, pillages, attacks on staff and patients.

The Status of Women and Girls in Congolese Society

Even before the war in Congo, women and girls were second class citizens. The law as well as social norms defined the role of women and girls as subordinate to men. Although women are often a major—if not the major—source of support for the family, the Congolese Family Code requires them to obey their husbands who are recognized as the head of the household.[38] Women and girls are also subordinate by custom and practice. A woman's status depends on being married and girls tend to marry at a young age. It is generally considered more important to educate boys than girls and a higher percentage of boys go to school than girls. Literacy statistics for Congo show how gender-specific discrimination was the norm before the war and continues to be a problem now.[39] Male household heads often settle violent crimes against women and girls outside the courts. Some have "resolved" rape cases by accepting a money payment from the perpetrator or his family or by arranging to have the perpetrator marry the victim. Because of the number of cases settled in this way and because of the reluctance of women to suffer the stigma of being known as rape victims, the cases officially reported are certainly far below the number of crimes actually committed. Women and girls who are raped suffer significant loss of social status, as discussed below. In cases of the death of women and girls by murder or negligence, the family of the victim sometimes agrees to accept the equivalent of a woman's bride price as compensation and does not pursue the case further.[40]

Given their subordinate status, women find it difficult to protect themselves against sexually transmitted diseases, in particular HIV/AIDS. Women cannot require their husbands to use condoms, and, as in many countries, extramarital sex for husbands (but not wives) is tolerated. The very large families that are a norm in Congo, especially in rural areas, tend to limit women's options for independence from their husbands.

---

[38] Code zaïrois de la famille, art. 444. See chapter IX. on the legal framework.

[39] In 1990 the net primary enrollment rate (percentage of age group) for boys was 61 percent and for girls 48 percent; in 1999 it was 33 percent for boys and 31 percent for girls (the 1999 percentages are the most recent data available within two years of 1999). The youth illiteracy rate (percentage of people aged 15-24) was 19 percent for boys and 42 percent for girls in 1990 compared with 12 percent for boys and 27 percent for girls in 1999. See Summary gender profile for the Democratic Republic of Congo located at http://genderstats.worldbank.org, accessed May 22, 2002).

[40] Speech by Immaculée Birhaheka at a workshop on documentation of sexual violence held on October 22, 2001, Goma. Human Rights Watch also learned of such cases during its interviews.

Outside the family, women likewise have limited power. Few Congolese women are in positions of leadership in civil society or in the political sphere. Although some effort was made to include women in the Inter-Congolese Dialogue, the vast majority of delegates are men.

Poverty and Survival Sex
The war has exhausted the reserves of the people of eastern Congo. The burden of trying to survive and assure that others in the family survive falls heavily on women. As the socio-economic situation worsens, more women and girls are resorting to trading sex for food, shelter, or money in order to provide for themselves and their families.[41]

Survival sex is different from the crimes of sexual violence committed by soldiers and combatants. But survival sex creates a context in which abusive sexual relationships are more accepted, and in which many men—whether civilian or combatant—regard sex as a "service" easy to get with the use of pressure.

Catherine B.,[42] a thirty-year-old widow and mother of eight, explained: "I do not dare to refuse men because I do not want to leave the children hungry."[43] In other cases girls without money for school fees have sex with their teachers in order to stay in school, or employees have sex with their employers in order to keep their jobs.[44] Sometimes women and girls in these situations are raped, but often they accept the sexual relationship reluctantly as a way of surviving. A woman who works for an organization for "girls in unfortunate circumstances" told us, "The war has pushed the girls to prostitution."[45] A U.N. official concurred. "We have come to the point where families even push their daughters into prostitution for simple survival," she said.[46] One woman said that she had no choice but to accept men who might leave her a bit of money, "for example 100 francs" ($.30), because she does not want her children to go hungry.[47]

---

[41] Human Rights Watch group interview, Goma, October 23, 2001.

[42] All names of victims and witnesses have been changed in order to protect their identity.

[43] Human Rights Watch interview, Goma, October 25, 2001.

[44] Human Rights Watch interviews, Bukavu October 17, 2001 and Goma, October 23, 2001.

[45] Human Rights Watch interview, Bukavu, October 19, 2001.

[46] Human Rights Watch interview with Gertrude Mudekereza, Program Assistant, World Food Programme, Bukavu, October 17, 2001.

[47] Human Rights Watch interview, Goma, October 25, 2001.

The exchange of sex for the necessities of life is apparently contributing to the spread of HIV/AIDS. "For a little money, for a little food, women give in," commented one doctor working in Goma.[48] As women and girls cannot insist that men use condoms, the risk of their contracting and passing on the HIV virus is increased dramatically.

Because of the circumstances and the frequency of their contacts with men outside their households, women and girls who engage in survival sex are at high risk of rape. One woman explained: "I have to keep doing bad things like sleeping with men to stay alive. You have to submit to everything they do, get slapped around, and then we're badly paid too."[49]

Many women living in RCD military camps, including widows of soldiers and women whose husbands are missing or away on duty, suffer sexual harassment and rape by soldiers and officers. They are sometimes forced to trade sex for being allowed to continue living in the camp. Some of these women also brew and sell alcoholic beverages to earn a small income. Soldiers who come to drink sometimes refuse to pay and sometimes rape the women. One widow served local beer to five RPA soldiers in March 2001. They refused to pay her and then raped her in front of her children.[50] One eighteen-year-old orphan who cares for younger brothers and sisters lives in a wrecked automobile on the grounds of a military camp. A local women's activist reported that she had sex with men who threatened otherwise to get her expelled from her shelter and the camp, and has been raped regularly by a RCD lieutenant who has a position of command at the camp.[51]

---

[48] Human Rights Watch telephone interview, Goma, October 26.

[49] Human Rights Watch interview, Bukavu, October 19, 2001.

[50] Human Rights Watch interview, Goma, October 25, 2001.

[51] Human Rights Watch interview, Goma, October 25, 2001.

SEXUAL VIOLENCE AS A WEAPON OF WAR

"There is real madness with all this [sexual] violence linked to the war. This is a whole war within the war—another kind of attack on the Congolese people," said a counselor who works with women and girls who have been subjected to rape and other forms of sexual violence.[52] Local observers remarked that such crimes increased in eastern Congo after the war began and particularly in the last year as the various warring parties contested control over such areas as that around the Kahuzi-Biega National Park, Shabunda territory, and the Uvira-Fizi region in South Kivu, particularly following RPA troop redeployments from Pweto,[53] as well as Masisi in North Kivu.

Sexual violence has been used as a weapon of war by most of the forces involved in this conflict. Combatants of the RCD, Rwandan soldiers, as well as combatants of the forces opposed to them—Mai-Mai, armed groups of Rwandan Hutu, and Burundian rebels of the Forces for the Defense of Democracy (Forces pour la défense de la démocratie, FDD) and Front for National Liberation (Front pour la libération nationale, FNL)—all frequently and sometimes systematically raped women and girls in the last year.

Soldiers and combatants raped and otherwise abused women and girls as part of their effort to win and maintain control over civilians and the territory they inhabited. They attacked women and girls as representatives of their communities, intending through their injury and humiliation to terrorize the women themselves and many others. One sixteen-year-old girl who was raped told us, "There is no way to protect girls from these things. I know they didn't target me—any [woman] would have had the same thing happen—but this is unacceptable. There are many girls who live in these conditions."[54]

This report focuses on crimes of sexual violence committed by soldiers and irregular combatants. But rape and other sexual crimes are not just carried out by members of armed factions but also increasingly by others in positions of authority and power, including the police, and by opportunistic common criminals and bandits, taking advantage of the prevailing climate of impunity and culture of violence to abuse women and girls.[55] For example in numerous

---

[52] Human Rights Watch interview with civil society activist, Bukavu, October 16, 2001.

[53] International Crisis Group, "Disarmament in the Congo: Investing in Conflict Prevention," Africa Briefing, June 12, 2001, p. 5.

[54] Human Rights Watch interview, Bukavu, October 19, 2001.

[55] In October 2001, a local human rights group in Goma found that four women had been raped in Goma prison. Human Rights Watch and local human rights groups have also registered cases of rape by police.

23

cases, soldiers, other combatants, and armed robbers raped women in the course of robbing and looting, sometimes after stealing everything they owned and sometimes to punish them if they had had no goods worth stealing. While the acts of ordinary criminals are not examined in detail in this report, cases are documented of attacks by armed men when there are indications that the perpetrators might have been combatants. Such an indication can be the language of the attackers; Kinyarwanda-speaking attackers are likely to be either members of Rwandan armed groups or of the RPA. If attackers are well-armed, this can also indicate a link to armed groups or forces of a regular army. Some cases fit into a pattern of abuse against civilians carried out by combatants, such as attacks on villagers by night or armed robberies in the city of Goma, and are therefore also documented.

Identifying Perpetrators

Women and girls who have been raped or otherwise attacked rarely identify the persons who committed the crimes. In many cases, the perpetrators were unknown to them and came from outside their communities. In other cases, particularly if the perpetrators believed they might be recognized, they tried to hide their identities by masking their faces or blinding the victims with lights. As one victim reported:

> There was no light. We didn't even have petrol to light a lamp, and the only light was when they shined the flashlight in our eyes. I couldn't see well what they were wearing. They wore masks and hats. We couldn't see their faces.[56]

Sometimes survivors and witnesses were able to identify the group of soldiers or combatants with whom the perpetrators were affiliated. They knew which groups had been operating in their region and where they were based. This allowed them to make identifications based partly on the location of the crime. In some cases survivors and witnesses knew perpetrators represented a certain group because they revealed their allegiance through what they said: Mai-Mai rapists, for example, accused victims of links with the RCD or the RPA. In other cases, survivors and witnesses drew conclusions based partly on the timing of the attack: RCD and RPA soldiers raped women in reprisal attacks on villages after they had been attacked shortly before by locally-based armed groups. When the physical appearance of the assailants appeared to correspond to that characteristic of an ethnic or national group, survivors and witnesses

---

[56] Human Rights Watch interview, Bukavu, October 18, 2001.

sometimes identified the perpetrators as having been of that group. Victims and witnesses sometimes relied on the language spoken by perpetrators and even on regional or other nuances of accent. In other cases, survivors and witnesses provided information about patterns of behavior that suggested identifications: Mai-Mai, for example, often held abducted women for very long periods of time, a year or more, while other combatants seemed more likely to release abductees after a shorter period. Mai-Mai also seemed more likely to require women to perform sexual acts for a number of combatants in the group, while perpetrators from other armed groups more frequently "allocated" abducted women to individuals.

In a significant number of cases women and girls who had been attacked recognized the difficulty of giving a positive identification and said only that their assailants were "armed men in uniform" or, simply, "men in uniform."[57] The uniforms worn by irregular combatants and soldiers are often similar, making it difficult to be sure which military unit or armed group is represented by the assailant. Physical appearances of assailants may also be insufficient to lead to identification based on the expected characteristic of one group and, even if such identification seems likely, it may in fact be wrong.[58] When RPA troops were predominantly Tutsi, local people ordinarily concluded that speakers of Kinyarwanda who looked stereotypically Hutu were not part of the RPA but rather members of armed groups opposed to the RPA or local Congolese of Rwandan extraction. With the increase in the numbers of Hutu RPA soldiers in eastern Congo, they can no longer draw such conclusions with accuracy.[59] Nor is language a sure indicator of group affiliation: many Congolese speak Kinyarwanda, for example.

In addition, perpetrators may try to confuse victims and witnesses by speaking languages that are not their habitual tongue. The counselor mentioned above commented, "There are military men who speak some Kinyarwanda to

---

[57] Human Rights Watch interview, Bukavu, October 16, 2001.

[58] The general perception is that Tutsi are tall and slim, and Hutu short and stocky. However this is a stereotype that often proves wrong.

[59] The U.N. special rapporteur on the situation on human rights in Congo reported that Hutu RPA soldiers were involved in massacre of sixty people, five of whom were burned alive, and in the rape of sixteen women and girls, some under the age of nine, in Chiherano, Bugobe, Nyatende, Kamisimbi, Lurhala and Nyangesi in South Kivu in December 2000 (Report of the Special Rapporteur on the Situation of Human Rights in Congo, pursuant to General Assembly resolution 55/117 and Commission on Human Rights resolution 2001/19, A/56/327, August 31, 2001, para. 80).

confuse people even if they are ordinarily Kiswahili speakers."[60] In other cases, Congolese speakers of Kinyarwanda allegedly sought to hide their identity by speaking with a Rwandan accent. In some cases, assailants warned those present during the attack to identify them as members of another group. One woman said that armed, Kiswahili-speaking, uniformed Congolese soldiers who attacked her daughter specifically instructed the girl to say that they were "Interahamwe" and not from the RCD.[61] According to the counselor who assists victims, they sometimes heed such warnings. He said, "Sometimes there may be cases of rape by the RCD but the girls say something else."[62]

In many places, individuals or small groups who have obtained arms commit crimes against local people, including crimes of sexual violence. Assailants include some who have deserted from one or another of the armed forces or groups of combatants operating in the region as well as others who have obtained firearms in other ways. A representative of a rural NGO assisting women told us that he and his colleagues used to think that it was Interahamwe who were responsible for rapes in their area, until it emerged that the attackers were soldiers, or Mai-Mai rebels, or deserters. He explained:

> But we found that it was the children of our village. We caught three of them. They had come to steal in the village and the villagers beat drums, so we caught them. They hide. They have weapons and know the place. Sometimes they are army deserters. Some are Mai-Mai, some are soldiers. Generally they are young people—the young people of the neighborhood. They do nothing. They like to be smart, to smoke dope.[63]

Given the difficulties of accurate identification of perpetrators, some victims, witnesses, and others simply attributed crimes to members of those groups which they themselves disliked. According to one human rights activist, "Many say 'Interahamwe' but it's hard to know if they are real or false

---

[60] Human Rights Watch interview with civil society activist, Bukavu, October 16, 2001.

[61] Human Rights Watch interview, Goma, October 25, 2001.

[62] Human Rights Watch interview with civil society activist, Bukavu, October 16, 2001.

[63] Human Rights Watch interview, Bukavu, October 17, 2001.

Interahamwe. There is confusion."[64] According to a Congolese lawyer, the RCD authorities also regularly attributed crimes to groups opposed to them. "Whenever there is something bad they blame it on the Mai-Mai or the Interahamwe."[65]

Such automatic and inaccurate accusations only ensure that many guilty assailants escape justice and encourage them and others to continue carrying out such crimes with impunity.

Sexual Violence in South Kivu

The larger cities and the main roads of South Kivu are controlled by Rwanda and the RCD but Mai-Mai forces and predominantly Hutu armed groups control or are fighting to control significant parts of the rest of the territory.

Near Kahuzi-Biega National Park

Rwandan Hutu rebel forces have been based in Kahuzi-Biega National Park for some time and have been accused of numerous attacks in adjacent areas, including in Bunyakiri, Kabare, Katana, and Walungu.[66] They have killed, raped, and pillaged the property of civilians whom they accuse of supporting the RCD or Rwandan government forces. RCD and Rwandan army forces wreak the same kind of violence on the same people, accusing them of assisting the Rwandan Hutu groups or the Mai-Mai.

Local residents say that attacks on civilians began after Rwandan refugees camps were destroyed in 1996 and the people who lived in them, including Interahamwe and ex-FAR, were scattered in the area. "We were fine during the time the refugees were here. But after the refugees left the camps, there were *abahinzi* (foreigners) and Interahamwe in the forest," said the representative of a women's organization whose members come from villages like Kajeje, Murhesa, and Kalonge, close to Kahuzi-Biega National Park.

In August 1998 Mathilde V. was in Chivanga, near Kavumu, when Rwandan Hutu combatants who said they were Interahamwe attacked the village at dawn as part of their ongoing struggle with RCD and RPA soldiers. "The Hutu had come to chase the Tutsi who occupied the area and who had just

---

[64] Human Rights Watch interview with civil society activist, Bukavu, October 16, 2001.

[65] Human Rights Watch interview, Bukavu, October 20, 2001.

[66] Surveyors trying to demarcate the park were killed in mid 2000. More recently, environmentalist organizations have highlighted the killings of gorillas, a protected species, in the park.

received supplies of ammunition," she explained. The assailants forced the women to line up and carry their loads of loot and ammunition to their base. Mathilde V. was two months pregnant and felt weak on the long walk towards Bunyakiri. The Interahamwe accused Mathilde V. of being the wife of a RCD or RPA soldier because she looked well-coiffed and well off and they accused others of having looted belongings from the refugee camps in 1996 and 1997. As the assailants accompanied the women down a path in the forest, they threw them to the ground and raped them. That day Mathilde V. and two others from her family were raped.

Following the rape she took traditional medicine believed to help pregnant women to protect themselves and the fetus if they suspected that their husbands had had another sexual partner. In her case, she took the medicine to protect herself against a sexually transmitted disease from the rape. When she later had difficulties in childbirth, she did not tell her doctor that she had been raped.[67]

Members of the predominantly Hutu armed groups preyed particularly upon women who passed near their forest bases as they were going to work in the fields, to collect firewood or charcoal, or to market. As a representative of the women's group said:

> For us, it's a three-hour walk from where we live to the forest. In Kalonge people live from [making and selling] charcoal. There are no vehicles for transporting charcoal.[68] It is usually transported on the backs of women...Women have to go through the forest when they're carrying charcoal or going for food and then they're attacked...now we live in fear.[69]

---

[67] Human Rights Watch interview, Bukavu, October 18, 2001.

[68] For security reasons, most vehicles avoid the boundaries of the Kahuzi-Biega National Park.

[69] Human Rights Watch interview with a representative of a women's organization, Murhesa, October 19, 2001. According to an association in Bukavu, women and girls are most vulnerable on market days. On some roads, they have to pass through roadblocks manned by the RCD, RPA or the Local Defense Force, an auxiliary force of the RCD composed of civilians. At some of the roadblocks they are required to give some of their charcoal as a toll. The total might amount to 60 FC (Congolese Francs), over a quarter of the cost of a bag of charcoal (200FC). A bag of charcoal sells for about 350 FC leaving a profit of about 100 FC, the equivalent of U.S. $.05 or two measures of manioc flour. To earn this amount from buying and selling charcoal costs each woman two days of traveling time and immeasurable personal risk.

Our team spoke with several women and girls in this area who had been abducted by armed Hutu, raped repeatedly, and forced to work for their captors. Générose N., from Kabare, aged twenty, told us what happened when she was on her way to visit her older sister:

> I was on the road from Kalonge to Mudaka. I had money that my fiancé gave me to buy a wedding dress. A soldier attacked me on the road. He said things in Kinyarwanda. [Later she said he was Hutu]. He took me away to a place in the forest where there were three other soldiers. They roughed me up.
>
> This was August 8 [2001] and they kept me until August 25 and each one of them raped me every day.
>
> There wasn't a house as such but a shelter under some plastic sheeting. I ate the things that they stole from time to time— *pâte* [a kind of cassava dough] made from stolen flour and sometimes meat. I found out that they had another woman there before me and I was sleeping where she slept, and then later they would get another woman after me. I wore the same clothes all the time.
>
> If I tried to speak, they hit me. They were all the same— horrible men.
>
> They finally just sent me away when they were tired of me. They took away the clothes I was wearing and gave me rags.
> I went to a health center that treats rape victims and got medicine. The Lord is the only one who can help me. He saved me from being killed; there is nowhere else to turn.
>
> They took my money for the wedding dress. My fiancé will still accept me even though now I have nothing. I didn't want to tell anyone about this, but I had to tell him because I was gone such a long time. And because I was gone such a long time, people talk about this even though I haven't told anyone else what happened.

Générose N. concluded that she did not see herself as particularly brave; "…it's just that I have no choice but to keep going. I don't have anything now," she said.[70]

In some cases armed assailants abducted women and girls in the course of robberies, forced them to carry the stolen goods to their bases, and then raped them there. Georgette W., mother of a six-year-old and a baby just a year and a half, related how she was abducted from Kajeje:

> It was an evening in June. I could hear that the soldiers [meaning armed men] were pillaging in the area. When they came to our house, I ran to protect myself. Every night they came around pillaging. But that night, after I ran, it started to rain. To get in from the rain, I decided to go back to the house.
>
> By then there were a lot of other people also seeking shelter from the rain—there were about eighteen of us, mostly neighbors and many old people. But the soldiers came and they were all around. There were a lot of them—I can't say how many; I could only hear their voices. I saw that everything in the house was stolen. My baby was on my back. Four combatants entered the house. They spoke Kinyarwanda. They were all armed. They took my baby away from me. I was the youngest woman in the house. They left the older women behind and took me.
>
> The four soldiers made me carry the things they had stolen on my back. Then later we met up with others and they gave the load on my back to a man they had captured. But I walked with the four who took me from the house. We walked in the forest from about 10 p.m. to midnight. I didn't know the place. Then I was alone with one of them. I later found out that the three others went off each with one woman they had captured.
>
> I was raped three times [by the one soldier]. He was armed the whole time. He didn't say anything and I didn't say anything. Finally he took off at about 3 in the morning. I was afraid to walk, but slowly I went back home and got there about 7:30.

---

[70] Human Rights Watch interview, Murhesa, October 19, 2001.

Asked how her husband treated her when she got home, Georgette W. replied:

> My husband didn't treat me badly. He was just worried about the diseases the soldier might have. I went and was tested and I didn't get any diseases. Our neighbors don't know about this. My husband told me not to say anything to anyone. He said, "Just tell people you were away for a short time."

Georgette W. said, "They hit me while we were walking, but they had already hit me at the house, so the neighbors already saw that [and were not surprised at her injuries]." She concluded: "I don't know why they did this. They took everything we had. . . all our things and our three goats, and they did this anyway."[71]

In May 2001, armed men attacked the village of Marie G., a twenty-year-old woman who was a charcoal seller from Kabare territory, and looted and burned many homes.[72] Marie G. fled, along with others. Having lost all her belongings, she went to Kalonge to get some charcoal to sell in order to buy clothes. When there she was abducted one night by three Rwandan members of a predominantly Hutu armed group who came to the house where she was staying at around 8 p.m. When Marie G. resisted being taken away, they beat her on the arm and shoulder, which still gave her pain when she was interviewed by our researchers five months later. She offered the assailants a goat if they would leave her alone but they turned down the offer saying they needed girls. She was joined by two girls who had been captured that same day while on their way to buy charcoal in Kalonge, Chantal R., aged seventeen, and Josephine A., aged eighteen, who were also interviewed by our team.[73] The assailants made them carry some of their stolen goods and walk with them to their forest camp where they arrived late at night. There they were told they had to cook and prepare a bed with grass and a sheet of plastic.

The three abductees said the men were called Lukala, Nyeka, and Vianney. They were dressed in civilian clothes and were armed with guns and machetes. Among themselves they spoke Kinyarwanda; with the girls they spoke Kiswahili.

---

[71] Human Rights Watch interview, Murhesa, October 19, 2001.

[72] Human Rights Watch interview, Murhesa, October 19, 2001.

[73] Human Rights Watch separate interviews at Murhesa, October 19, 2001.

Each of the combatants took one of them. It was Lukala who demanded sex from Marie G. and told her that if she did not "give herself" to him, she would have to stay with them. She refused. Lukala told her: "You are no better than my wife and she was shot dead." Marie G. answered that he should just kill her. She heard the other two girls screaming. "I heard my companions crying," she said, "so I refused. The man said to me, 'They have already begun working—why are you creating problems for me?'" He slapped her and after her companions called out to her, "Accept it; there's nothing you can do," and he raped her for the first of many times.

"So I let him do it. He made me suffer greatly," Marie G. said and continued that she asked him why he made others suffer. "He answered, "That is the job of a soldier." He told Marie G. that he had had many women but that none was as terrible (that is, resistant) as she was. He threatened to shoot her and after several hours began to rape her again. He raped her five times during the first night.

After that night, Vianney, leader of the group, also wanted to "have" her. After a dispute with Lukala over this, she spent the second night with Vianney. He told her that he was going to be much nicer to her than Lukala and that she only would have to sleep with him once per night and could then sleep. She told him it was not easy for her to sleep in the circumstances.

Frightened and afraid of being traced later, Marie G. did not give them her real name. She also lied to her captors, claiming that she had two children, and begged to be released. Vianney told her he could release her only if Lukala agreed. She appealed to Vianney's moral sense by telling him that he would not want members of his own family treated this way. The assailants let Marie G. go after three days and kept one of her companions for five days and the other for a week.[74]

A short time later, in early June 2001, the same three assailants captured two young women, eighteen-year-old Cécile K. and twenty-year-old Béatrice K. in a nighttime raid on their home and held them for two to three weeks. Béatrice K. said she hid under her bed when her home was attacked but that the men found her by using their flashlights. They accused her of being a "friend of the Tutsi." They told her they had had to leave their families behind in Rwanda but that she was still fortunate enough to have her parents. "When I cried, they hit me," she said.[75] A week or so after their capture, the assailants abducted seventeen-year-old Valerie J. from her home. When she cried, they told her,

---

[74] Human Rights Watch interview, Murhesa, October 19, 2001.

[75] Human Rights Watch interview, Bukavu, October 18, 2001.

"You are not going to change the situation with your tears. You are not more important than those we have left behind in Rwanda."[76]

The captors raped the girls repeatedly and made them cook and do other household work. It appears that this group of men had abducted many women and girls before, one of them claiming that they had had forty women.[77] At one stage they took Valerie J., Béatrice K. and Cécile K. to find other women or girls for them but the village they went to was deserted and so none was taken. According to Béatrice K., escape was impossible because they were guarded all the time and they did not know where they were. Three weeks after the capture of Beatrice and Cecile and one week after Valerie J. was taken, one of the captors released the girls because his two companions had been killed. Marie G. said that she had heard that the two had "been killed by Tutsi on the road to Kalonge." Cécile K. said that "Tutsi soldiers" later came to her village and told her they had killed the third man.

According to the girls, the three men said they were receiving orders from a "commander" but they believed this was a ruse to intimidate them. The three men were never together with any others and had no radios or mobile phones, which indicates that they might have been acting independently of other Hutu forces in the area. Over a period of several weeks, they moved several times within the forest, perhaps because they were aware that RCD troops were pursuing them.

A representative of a women's organization explained that sexual violence had increased recently, in part because assailants found little to rob from people who had been repeatedly attacked, and wanted to punish them as a result for their perceived lack of support.

> Various armed bands have been through our area; there has been a great deal of pillaging...people are really left with nothing and in some cases they have been displaced. Since there is nothing left to steal, the armed bands have taken up this systematic rape....There were rapes before this year, but people didn't talk about it. Finally it got to be so much that we went to the parish and with its help, we have had the courage to speak about this.[78]

---

[76] Human Rights Watch interview, Murhesa, October 19, 2001.

[77] Human Rights Watch interview, Murhesa, October 19, 2001.

[78] Human Rights Watch interview with a representative of a women's organization, Murhesa, October 19, 2001.

Twenty-five-year-old Elisabeth S. from Walungu territory was raped by
armed men who came to rob her home in January 2001. She said,

> It started at 1 a.m. We were all sleeping. I heard the noise and
> was the first to wake up. There were ten of them—I could see
> them and count them. They came into the compound. I wanted
> to hide but I couldn't. They said, "Give us your money." Then
> they said, "Get us your father" and told me to wake everyone
> up. I told them there was no one here. But then my father got
> up and turned on the flashlight. The combatants could see the
> light and said, "Who's that with the flashlight?" Two of the
> combatants who were very well armed were near me. I don't
> know how, but my father was able to escape by running very
> fast between the two of them. One said to me, "We're going to
> kill you for letting him get away."
>
> The leader told the others to shoot Papa. We were all praying.
> I thought they were going to kill us all too. My mother didn't
> know whether to run with Papa. But she hid under the bed and
> was praying with her rosary. Mama was able to run and got
> away when some other soldiers came into the house.
>
> They kept me, my two sisters, and another girl who was
> staying with us sitting on the ground outside—there were two
> of them watching us. There was another one in the house.
> They took everything and asked us what else the family had.
> We said the only thing left is the clothes we are wearing;
> everything else is in the house. They left the goats and
> chickens but took everything else.
>
> I thought if the Lord says it's our time, this is when we will
> die. The combatants said, "We can kill you," and shot in the
> air four times to show what they could do. There was another
> girl who stayed with us, an orphan, who usually slept with me,
> but she was alone in another small house that night. She saw
> us outside, but somehow she didn't see the combatants. I
> could see her coming slowly toward us and I wondered what
> she was doing. I couldn't keep her from coming—she came up
> to us slowly and then said, "What is happening?" Even though

the moon was bright, she still didn't see the combatants. But they saw her, and they caught her and beat her, kicked her, and whipped her with a rope. She said she would rather be killed than suffer with them. But then they threw her on the ground with the rest of us.

The assailants then raped each of the five girls. The youngest was fourteen years old.

Each combatant took one of us to one of the small houses outside the compound. There was no way to resist. They spoke Kinyarwanda and Lingala—they were both Congolese and Interahamwe. They gave themselves names like Kofi and Bamba. It didn't take too long.

I think they didn't need to kill us; they did what they wanted to do. They stole everything and went away at about 4 a.m.. Then Papa came home. We thought he was dead, so when we saw him, we were so happy. None of the shots had hit him. We stayed home the rest of that night, but the next night no one would sleep there.

I go back to our village sometimes, but I don't sleep well when I'm there. The neighbors know that we were robbed, but they don't know about what happened to me.[79]

While combatants opposed to the RCD are most often accused of the sexual violence reported around Kahuzi-Biega National Park, RCD soldiers have also attacked women and girls. Bijou K., a young mother, told us that she was raped by a Kinyarwanda-speaking RCD soldier on a road in Kabare territory. She said:

This was in June 2001. I left my house in the evening to buy food for my children. A soldier attacked me and pushed me off the road. He asked me in Kinyarwanda for my identity card. He wore a uniform and had a rifle.

He threw me into the bushes. My baby, who was one month and one week old, was on my back. He threw the baby off my

---

[79] Human Rights Watch interview, Bukavu, October 18, 2001.

back—the baby was on his stomach on the ground—and put a gun to my chest.

When I reached to save my baby, he took off my clothes and raped me. It happened fast; he wasn't there a long time. Afterwards, he took off.

I picked up the baby and went home. I told my husband what happened. I had just had a baby and I needed help. I was treated [at a clinic]. It turns out that I got a sexually transmitted disease, and now my husband has it too. I also have skin rashes, and I'm using local medicine for that.

I don't think I was especially targeted by this soldier. So many other people have been attacked too.[80]

Fifteen-year-old Jeanette T. described how soldiers whom she described as Tutsi kidnapped her sisters in Ngwesha outside Bukavu:

It was April 25, 2001. I was in the village with my family. My father had sold a chicken. Men came during that same night and told him to give them the money from selling the chicken. Our family [Jeanette T., her parents, and her three unmarried sisters, aged between eighteen and twenty-two] was all around the fire. They cut my father with knives. There were lots of them. Our whole compound was full of soldiers. They had knives and guns. They spoke some Lingala and some Kinyarwanda. They raped my sisters and my mother, but I was able to run. They took everything that was in our house. I hid behind some trees on a hill a bit above the house.

They took away my sisters and we still don't know where they are. There were five or six men with each of my sisters. The next morning I went back to the house. I found my father there still injured with a neighbor who was trying to help him. After three days, my mother came back. But we still don't know where my sisters are.

---

[80] Human Rights Watch interview, Murhesa. October 19, 2001.

My father wanted to go and find them and tried to get help, but the neighbors said that he if did that the Tutsi would exterminate the whole family. Now we are in Bukavu and some of the family of our old neighbors have helped us a little but we don't even have clothes. There was no reason to target my father who is a good Christian man. We will keep asking people about whether they have seen my sisters.[81]

The data gathered by our researchers on rape and other sexual abuse in the area around the Kahuzi-Biega National Park was consistent with that collected independently by two local human rights organizations. The Congolese women's rights association PAIF registered sixty-nine cases of rape by predominantly Hutu armed bands and by RCD soldiers in the Irhambi-Katana area of Kabare territory between May 1999 and September 2001. A second organization reported that "men in uniform identified as Interahamwe" killed, raped, and pillaged so frequently in villages near the Kahuzi-Biega National Park that residents had abandoned their homes to sleep outside in the search for security.[82]

Shabunda Territory

Shabunda town, 350 kilometers southwest of Bukavu in the territory of Shabunda, is strategically located for controlling the east of the province and its vast mineral wealth. The town is surrounded on three sides by the Ulindi River, beyond which thick equatorial forest stretches for hundreds of kilometers. Residents of the town, like people who inhabit nearby villages, depend on the forest for most of the necessities of life: they grow crops and hunt and gather food and firewood there. Given the distance from other centers and the poor state of the roads, Shabunda imports few supplies from the outside and those brought in usually come by air. Mai-Mai and Hutu armed groups have fought the RCD and their RPA allies for control of this region since late 1998. With the ongoing conflict the town has become increasingly isolated. In late 2001 it had the atmosphere of an embattled fortress.

Mai-Mai have been able to occupy the town only occasionally and briefly, such as in early 2000, but they control much of the surrounding forest. As the U.N. Office for the Coordination of Humanitarian Affairs (OCHA) said,

---

[81] Human Rights Watch interview, Bukavu, October 19, 2001.

[82] PAIF, "Enquete sur les cas de blessés suite à la guerre;" Centre pour la Paix et les Droits de l'Homme-Peace and Human Rights Center (CPDH-PHaC), "Occasionnel d'Information et Revendication du CPDH-PHRC," No 017 du 03 mai 2001.

"Shabunda town is the only place, in the whole territory where one has access to population without the danger of interference from armed bands."[83]

As fighting increased in early 1999, nearly half the population of Shabunda town fled—most of it to the forest—reducing the number of inhabitants from more than 32,000 in 1998 to 17,600 in early 1999. Residents of nearby villages also sought refuge in the forest.[84] One international humanitarian association working in the area estimated that between 60 and 80 percent of the displaced persons are in households headed by women.[85]

In their struggle to control territory, each side used violence, including violence against women and girls, to win or keep control over the local population. Residents who fled to the forest when the Mai-Mai advanced hesitated to return afterwards to homes in areas where the RCD had regained control, fearing the RCD would see them as supporters of the Mai-Mai and take reprisals against them. Others wished to return home but feared attack by Mai-Mai if they tried to do so. To hurry their return, the RCD reportedly announced in a public meeting that civilians who did not come back from the forest would be considered enemies and subject to attack. For a period the RCD soldiers prohibited town residents from going to cultivate fields and to gather food and wood in the forest—or limited the times when they could do so—apparently hoping thus to impede any collaboration between them and the Mai-Mai.[86]

In March 2001 RCD troops organized a Local Defense Force, an armed, minimally-trained paramilitary force that is recruited in the area and continues to live at home while carrying out patrols and other military duties. Each household in the community is required to contribute two glassfuls of rice every two days to support the Local Defense Force.[87] During 2001 RCD troops and members of the Local Defense Force started going into the forest to find and escort groups of displaced persons to their homes or to new locations designated

---

[83] U.N. OCHA South-Kivu, "Rapport de mission Shabunda," May 2001, p2. U.N. OCHA states that Shabunda territory is the largest in South Kivu, and extends to 25,216 square kilometers.

[84] U.N. Office for the Coordination of Humanitarian Affairs (OCHA) South-Kivu, Rapport de mission Shabunda, May 2001, p3.

[85] Norwegian Refugee Council IDP database, 2001, quoted in Save the Children, Oxfam and Christian Aid, "No End In Sight, The human tragedy of the conflict in the Democratic Republic of Congo," August 2001, p10.

[86] See Human Rights Watch, "Eastern Congo Ravaged," p. 17.

[87] Human Rights Watch group interview, Shabunda, October 21, 2001. A force with the same name and functions operates in Rwanda. The organization was likely introduced into the region by RPA troops.

by the RCD authorities. Those who wanted to leave the forest but feared Mai-Mai attack welcomed the assistance of the RCD and the Local Defense Force.[88]

Shabunda town is exceptional for the number of women and girls who have admitted publicly to having been raped, most of them by Mai-Mai. The governor of South Kivu estimated that 2,500 to 3,000 women and girls had been raped between late 1999 and mid-2001 and a religious congregation reported having assisted some 2,000 raped women and girls.[89] International aid workers active in the area told our researchers that such figures were plausible and probably underestimated. As one humanitarian aid worker commented: "Whatever the number, it's a systematic pattern of abuse."[90] According to many local and international observers, it is not the number of rapes but rather the willingness of the victims to talk about them which is unique to Shabunda; they believe that the crimes are as widespread elsewhere in eastern Congo but remain partly hidden by the continuing reluctance of women to speak out.

"In Shabunda [town], the women have had the courage to speak out. In other places they don't," a nurse with an international agency who has worked extensively in South Kivu told us.[91] One of the reasons cited for this relative openness is that many women and girls were raped in the presence of others. Family members, friends, or other captured women were forced to watch. In several cases, children were reportedly forced to hold their mothers down while they were raped. In addition, many women abducted by the Mai-Mai were held for long periods, up to a year and a half. Women and girls returning home after being held for so long were generally assumed to have been raped and most saw no reason to pretend otherwise. Other women and girls came back with obvious injuries that could only have been inflicted in sexual assaults. Sometimes women and girls were raped with objects such as sticks of wood and hot peppers.[92] Many women and girls required medical attention for prolapsed

---

[88] Human Rights Watch interview, Shabunda, October 21, 2001.

[89] The figure of 2,500 to 3,000 victims, given by the governor, seemed to refer to South Kivu province as a whole. UN OCHA, "Compte rendu de la commission ESPD sur les femmes violées de Shabunda", July 2001, p.1, and UN OCHA South-Kivu, "Rapport de Mission Shabunda", May 2001, p.4. Also Human Rights Watch interviews with representatives of the International Rescue Committee, Bukavu, October 15 and 17, 2001, and Médecins Sans Frontières, Bukavu, October 16, 2001, and Goma, October 24, 2001; and other interviews in Bukavu and Shabunda, October, 2001.

[90] Human Rights Watch interview with staff of the International Rescue Committee, Bukavu, October 15, 2001.

[91] Human Rights Watch interview, Bukavu, October 17, 2001.

[92] Human Rights Watch interviews with Guy Cirhuza, Humanitarian Assistant, UN OCHA, and Gertrude Mudekereza, Program Assistant, World Food Programme, Bukavu,

uteruses, severe vaginal tears and fistulas.[93] Some women and girls also became pregnant as a result of having been raped.

Other circumstances have apparently contributed to the willingness of women and girls in Shabunda to speak about rapes and other sexual abuse which they have suffered. A support group assists victims, one of the few operating in the region, and an international aid organization has experimented with treating women and girls free of charge for rape-related injuries and complications. RCD authorities see political advantage in drawing attention to rapes and other abuses committed by their opponents. The governor of the province has encouraged humanitarian organizations and journalists to examine the problem. The majority of women and girls described those who raped them as "Mai-Mai," a term which can mean simply members of the local population. As a priest from the territory of Shabunda commented: "Who are the Mai-Mai? They are the people from here...the youth from around here, the Interahamwe. All are Mai-Mai against the invaders—the RCD."[94] While Mai-Mai may be "against the invaders," this does not necessarily mean they seek to protect the local population—sometimes the opposite—particularly if they believe the local population has cooperated with the RCD.

Sophie W., a mother in her mid-thirties, said she was taken by Mai-Mai in July, 2000 and was held for over a year with her four children, aged six, ten, and thirteen, and a baby who was still breast-feeding. She told us that her family was targeted in part because the Mai-Mai thought her husband was linked with the RCD:

> We went into the forest at the beginning of the war. My
> husband thought the forest was safer, and there was nothing to
> eat in town. But we moved back to town in 2000. In July 2000
> the Mai-Mai came and took my husband. They beat me up

October 17, 2001; with Cory Kik, Médecins Sans Frontières, Bukavu, October 16, 2001; with International Rescue Committee, Bukavu, October 15 and 17, 2001; and other interviews in Bukavu and Shabunda, October 2001.

[93] A fistula is an abnormal connection that develops between two of the body's organs. Recto-vaginal fistulas connect the rectum and the vagina and result in fecal matter passing through the fistula to the vagina and thus are often accompanied by fecal incontinence and infections; vesico-vaginal fistulas connect the vagina and the bladder and may result in urinary incontinence and infections. Fistulas develop from injury such as trauma or severe inflammation due to a disease. Some fistulas will close spontaneously; others require surgical intervention.

[94] Human Rights Watch interview, Shabunda, October 22, 2001.

and shot him and then cut up his body in front of me. They said my husband was a spy for the Tutsi.

There were eight Mai-Mai. Two of them held me down and the others raped me. They put two knives to my eyes and told me that if I cried, they would cut out my eyes.

The Mai-Mai spoke Kiswahili, Kilenga, Lingala, and Kinyarwanda. They were filthy—they had fleas. We had no shelter. There were only leaves to sleep on, and when it rained, we got soaked. We had mats with us, but the Mai-Mai took them away. There were many of them during the time I was in the forest—even 150 or more. They sometimes fed us small animals that they killed, but they didn't give us much food.[95]

Mai-Mai sometimes killed and raped local people who it held had shown an acceptance of RCD authority by leaving the forest. In one such case in early September 2001, Mai-Mai attacked a group who had left the forest shortly before under RCD escort and who were gathered for worship in a church in a Masanga village, about forty kilometers from Shabunda. Natalie R., a survivor of the attack who was herself raped, told us that forty-three bodies were found in the vicinity after the attack. She had been in the forest with her family near Minoro, a village about fifty-five kilometers from Shabunda. Her husband had been taken a year previously by the Mai-Mai and she has not seen him since:

After we had been near Minoro for about two years, the RCD came and took a lot of the families who were in the forest and resettled us in Masanga. In our case, a boy who knew us told the RCD where we were and they came to find us. But before they settled us in Masanga, the RCD pillaged our homes and took everything.

We were in Masanga a short time—maybe two weeks—when a lot of the Christian families who had been in the forest went to the early mass at Masanga parish. We had been in the forest a long time and were looking forward to going to mass.

---

[95] Human Rights Watch interview, Shabunda, October 22, 2001.

This was the 8:30 a.m. mass. I was there with my five children, but only the three girls came inside. The two boys were hanging around outside with some other children. It was about 10:30 and the church was still full. All of a sudden we heard shots coming from all over. Some were individual shots, but there was one automatic weapon. [She imitated the sound of it.] Four people were shot in the church—two women and two children.

There were a lot of Mai-Mai outside the church. People tried to run, but there was such a panic that the door was blocked by the crowd. Some people did manage to run. Of those, some escaped to the forest, which is close to Masanga. Some were shot but managed to get to the forest where they died. Some were shot near the church or died before they got to the forest. When we went to collect the dead after the Mai-Mai left, we found twenty-seven dead in the forest and twelve dead near the church in addition to the four who were killed in the church. My two sons managed to flee, and they were not hurt.

After some people ran, six Mai-Mai came into the church. They were armed. They wore uniforms and masks and had animal skins on their heads. They were very dirty. There were some Batembo, some Bakongo, and some Bahutu.[96] There were not many of us left in the church by then—four women, three older women, and me—and some children. The soldiers raped all four of us. They hit me with a stick twice. They said we were stupid for obeying the RCD and said they would save the Congolese people. They were in the church for about thirty minutes and then took off.

The other women who were raped were old, and they can't speak of it. I have no one to help me, and I have nothing left. There is no health facility in Masanga, so I couldn't get medical help. I still have a lot of pain, but I am menstruating [indicating that she does not believe she is pregnant].[97]

---

[96] The Batembo and Bahutu (or Hutu) are ethnic groups in eastern Congo. In this quotation, "Bakongo" probably means Congolese as opposed to Rwandan.

[97] Human Rights Watch interview, Shabunda, October 22, 2001.

Mai-Mai preyed upon women who sought safety by moving temporarily to the forest as well as those who remained in town but continued to go to the forest to cultivate, seek food, or make charcoal to keep themselves and their families alive.[98] At one time RCD troops required local people to gather firewood for them and this too forced women to take the risk of going into the forest.[99]

A U.N. official said that women and girls in Shabunda, like those who live from the charcoal trade in Kahuzi-Biega National Park "are very vulnerable for reasons having to do with livelihood and survival. They are the ones who go looking for wood, food, fruits, and they are taken when they are doing that. But they have to keep doing it even after they are raped."[100] And after being displaced and often unable to cultivate normally for three seasons, the population is desperate.[101]

Solange C., a fifty-year-old mother of four, was working in her field in the forest with her children and her mother when they were attacked early one morning in April 2000.

> There were seven men with us too, helping to work the fields. A group of Mai-Mai came upon us. The men heard them coming and they all ran.
>
> There were eight of them. They made a circle around me. They held my feet up and opened my legs and raped me. They said that if they found the men who ran away, they would eat them.
>
> The two men in charge were wearing uniforms. The others were in dirty rags. They had animal skins and feathers on their heads, and around their neck they carried the drug that they say makes them strong. I could really only see their eyes; everything else was hidden. They acted crazy as though they were drugged.

---

[98] Human Rights Watch interviews, Bukavu, October 20, 2001, and Shabunda, October 21 and 22, 2001.

[99] Human Rights Watch interview, Bukavu, October 16, 2001.

[100] Human Rights Watch interview with Guy Cirhuza, Humanitarian Assistant, U.N. OCHA, Bukavu, October 17, 2001.

[101] U.N. OCHA South-Kivu, Rapport de mission Shabunda, May 2001, p4.

Solange C. explained that the attackers took everything from her little banana leaf shelter in the forest. Her neighbors came to her assistance when they heard that the Mai-Mai had gone. She took some traditional medicines from the forest that her mother knew of, "the kind they give to girls who are just beginning to menstruate." That helped a bit, she said, but she continues to have pain. She continued to live in the forest for one year and one month and on occasion was obliged to labor for the Mai-Mai. Describing her living conditions during that time Solange C. said:

> I ate manioc during that time or leaves without any oil or salt. I used papaya leaves [to wash myself] because there was no soap. They [the Mai-Mai] were full of fleas, so we got fleabites and scabies. We just slept on leaves with no shelter. Sometimes we had a fire to keep us warm. The children got sick and I gave them medicines that I could find in the forest. Only the strength of God saved us during all this. Finally, the Local Defense Force and the RCD found some other people and then found my family. Somebody told them where we were—and they said that when we heard gunfire, we should follow the sound and come to them. That's what we did. About thirty people came out with us in that way."[102]

Our research team also spoke with a man whose wife had been taken by the Mai-Mai in June of 2001. He remains in Shabunda with their two young children. His wife has not been seen since but some other women who had likewise been kidnapped had escaped with the help of the Local Defense Force and the RCD and gave him news of his wife. They told him that she had been taken by the Mai-Mai even deeper into the forest.[103]

In addition, some of the women and girls of Shabunda said that their assailants had been young men from local villages or bandits from the area who simply used the name Mai-Mai to cover their crimes. In June 2001 Angélique H. was raped on her way to work her field near her village about forty kilometers from Shabunda. She referred to the three rapists as Mai-Mai but also said that she recognized them as coming from her village. She said: "Everyone is Mai-

---

[102] Human Rights Watch interview, Shabunda, October 22, 2001.

[103] Human Rights Watch interview, Shabunda, October 22, 2001.

Mai. At the beginning they were good, but then they became bad."[104] In April 2001 Lisa T. was raped by five men she called Mai-Mai when she went to her field to get manioc. She did not know them but said that they were "boys from the village." She said that she dared not accuse them because one day they could come after her if she did.[105]

Several witnesses told us that RCD and RPA soldiers had also committed rapes but that no one dared speak openly about them.[106] Although the authorities encourage reporting of rapes perpetrated by the Mai-Mai or by predominantly Hutu armed groups, they do not encourage reports about violence committed by their own or their patron's troops. In some cases, the civilian authorities themselves fear the RCD and the Rwandan army, which have a strong presence in Shabunda town. As a resident of Shabunda told our team, "The allies justify their presence by what is going on. The authorities don't want the Rwandans here but they don't have the courage to say so. No authority is capable of leading—they have no conscience."[107]

Uvira and Fizi Territories

For several years RCD forces and their allies, the Rwandan and Burundian armies, have battled Mai-Mai and the Burundian rebel forces, FDD and FNL, for control of Fizi and Uvira territories. The RCD, RPA, and Burundian army units allied to them control parts of the plain along Lake Tanganyika and the Rusizi River, including the city of Uvira, some towns to its north, and the main road linking these points. Mai-Mai and their allies have kept the RCD out of most of the mountainous area of Uvira and Fizi territories. The RCD nominally controls the highlands inhabited by the Banyamulenge, but it recently fought a rebellion led by a Banyamulenge militia in this region.

The warring parties currently fight over much of the region from Uvira south to Fizi along Lake Tanganyika, an area which has been contested for some time. Local human rights organizations have reported serious violations of international humanitarian law, including naval bombardment of villages along the lakeshore by Burundian government forces allied to the RCD, and massacres of civilians.[108]

---

[104] Human Rights Watch interview, Shabunda, October 22, 2001.

[105] Human Rights Watch interview, Shabunda, October 22, 2001.

[106] Human Rights Watch interviews, Shabunda and Bukavu, October, 2001.

[107] Human Rights Watch interview, Shabunda, October 22, 2001.

[108] The best known incident is the massacre in Makobola, January 1999; another grave incident was the massacre of civilians in Lusende, July 2000.

Because contending forces sometimes seek to demonstrate control over the roads by ambushing travelers, residents of the area travel less now than in the past. Women and girls are the main local traders. Afraid of rape as well as death should they venture along the roads, they have almost stopped trading between Uvira and Fizi as well as between Uvira and the mid-plateau. Fewer locally produced goods from Fizi, such as manioc, charcoal, palm nuts, and fish reach Uvira and fewer imported goods from Uvira, such as gas, clothes, sugar, beer, soap, and salt are delivered to Fizi. Salt and soap are in short supply in some areas. Fishing activities on the lake have decreased because equipment has been looted and many fishermen have left or been killed. The number of widows and orphans has risen. With the decrease in trade and a corresponding decrease in income, fewer families can afford to send their children to school; many can only afford to eat once a day.[109]

In mid-2001 RPA troops redeployed from Pweto led more vigorous fighting against Mai-Mai and the Burundian rebel group FDD[110] which, working out from its base on the Ubwari peninsula, had taken towns between Uvira and Fizi and controlled much of the road in between the two cities. In early September, Mai-Mai forces advanced towards Fizi and occupied the city for several weeks with the help of the FDD and FNL. By October the RCD had retaken Fizi and other towns to the south, driving back the Mai-Mai forces. Thousands of displaced persons fled to Baraka and Uvira and others crossed the border to Tanzania.

As elsewhere in eastern Congo, the number of rapes in this region increased with the surge in military activities. Among persons displaced by combat between RCD and Mai-Mai and FDD forces beginning in mid-2001, women and girls from Swima, Mboko, Kabumbe and Kazimia reported having been raped during or soon after military engagements. For example one elderly woman said her daughter-in-law was raped in August 2001 by three soldiers whom she described as "Banyamulenge" when they tried to return to their home in Kabumbe after having fled combat between RCD and Mai-Mai.[111]

Thirty-eight-year-old Viviane M. left Kabumbe on October 23, 2001 because of continued fighting between the RCD and the Mai-Mai. Mai-Mai attacked an RCD position and then entered the village and began looting the houses. Viviane M. fled with her family as RCD reinforcements were bought in

---

[109] Human Rights Watch group interview, Uvira, November 1, 2001.

[110] International Crisis Group, "Disarmament in the Congo: Investing in Conflict Prevention," Africa Briefing, June 12, 2001, p. 5; and Ninth Report of the Secretary-General on the U.N. Organization Mission in DR Congo, S/2001/970, paragraph 23.

[111] Human Rights Watch interview, Uvira, November 1, 2001.

from nearby positions. Hiding in the forested area in the hills above the town, she heard sounds of combat for several days. Some Mai-Mai forces took advantage of the vulnerability of the displaced people and robbed them of everything of value. In the following days Mai-Mai found where they were hiding and raped the girls and women. Viviane M. described how a group of Mai-Mai demanded that she give them all her money. Upon discovering that she had nothing, they stripped off her clothing, beat her with the butts of their rifles, and three of them raped her in succession. Some of them raped her fourteen-year- old daughter before her eyes.[112]

Marceline G. also fled Kabumbe during the same period. During her stay in the forest, some Mai-Mai forces located their hiding place and forced the men to accompany them to loot an abandoned village nearby. During their absence, other Mai-Mai and FDD combatants raped the women and girls who were left behind and beat some of them with clubs and rifles. Several witnesses testified that the forces were under a Mai-Mai leader named Bwasakala.[113]

Between July and September 2001, a human rights organization from Uvira registered 117 cases of sexual violence against women and girls. Most of the attacks occurred in Fizi territory during recent fighting and most were perpetrated by FDD or RCD forces. The victims included girls as young as eleven years old, several pregnant women, and elderly women. The organization also documented several cases in which women were shot because they protested the rape of their daughters. According to the organization, RCD soldiers raped and then killed five women on August 5, 2001 in Lusambo, fifteen kilometers north of Mboko, in Fizi territory.[114]

Another association reported rapes of women and girls by RCD troops and FDD and Mai-Mai combatants in the villages of Kabumbe, Kalundja, Lusambo, Swima and Munene. Some of the women were raped in front of their husbands and/or their children, and some were killed after the rape. As in the cases above, many of the rapes were perpetrated on displaced women and soon after military engagements.[115] Local human rights groups have also reported that RCD, Banyamulenge, FDD, Burundian army, and RPA forces have raped women and girls in and around Uvira. Some of the women and girls became pregnant after

---

[112] Human Rights Watch Interview, Uvira, October 31, 2001.

[113] Human Rights Watch Interview, Uvira, October 31, 2001.

[114] Report by local human rights group in Uvira, unpublished.

[115] Report about the situation in Fizi territory by a local human rights organization in Uvira, unpublished.

the rape, and some had miscarriages.[116] Several local observers in Uvira commented that incidents of sexual violence were more frequent in areas controlled by the RCD than those occupied by their Burundian allies.[117]

Soldiers and other combatants also attacked and raped women whom they found in their fields. On May 20, 2001, RCD soldiers raped Linette P., a forty-three-year-old peanut seller and divorced mother of two. She had gone to her field where she cultivates manioc, corn, and peanuts towards Kiliba (north of Uvira). It had looked like rain so few others had gone to cultivate. She was alone when she left the field in the middle of the afternoon and was set upon by soldiers who came from the mountains where they had been fighting. "They said, 'Come here, we have spent many days without women, you are going to be our wife,'" Linette P. related. Two of the soldiers raped her in the field and then climbed into a military vehicle with the others and drove away.[118]

Albertine W., an eighteen-year-old with two children, was raped by an RCD soldier in August 2001 near Mboko, Fizi territory. She was working in the field with her mother-in-law when the soldier approached and raped her. She said, "It went very quickly, and the soldier did not otherwise abuse me." She reported that many other women and girls were also raped by RCD soldiers. As a consequence, the family decided to leave their village and go into the mountains, which are controlled by the Mai-Mai.[119]

Colette F., a forty-five year old mother of nine, was raped three years ago by two soldiers in her field in Munanira, about 5 kilometers from Uvira. At about 8 a.m., she suddenly saw many people running and four soldiers coming down a hill. When the soldiers caught up to her, they told her and another woman to come carry their baggage. As she and the other woman approached, the soldiers grabbed them, threw them down, and raped them. One of the soldiers held her at gunpoint while the other raped her. Each of the two women was raped by two soldiers who then told them, "If you tell this in the village, we will kill you." Colette F. believes that the assailants were Banyamulenge or Rwandan—she said she cannot tell the difference. Asked about judicial redress, she answered: "Here you can't take [these things] to court. There are those who are strong, and we are scared of them."[120]

---

[116] Reports by a local human rights organization in Uvira, unpublished.

[117] Human Rights Watch interviews, Uvira, November 1-2, 2001.

[118] Human Rights Watch interview, Uvira, October 31, 2100.

[119] Human Rights Watch interview, Uvira, November 1, 2001.

[120] Human Rights Watch interview, Uvira, October 31, 2001.

Burundian Hutu rebels have reportedly abducted Congolese girls and women to provide them with sexual services and daily labor in their camps, including those in the Rukoko, a forested area in the Rusizi plain, on the Burundian side of the border. Twenty-year-old Agathe T. managed to escape such a fate. She said that the rebels often attack her home area of Nyango, twelve kilometers from Sange. They come looking for money and beat people up if they have nothing to give them, she said, and sometimes they take women and girls away with them. In early October 2001, Burundian Hutu rebels, in uniform and speaking Kirundi, tried to kidnap Agathe T. but she managed to escape through a window. They caught and raped other women and girls, among them her eighteen-year-old sister who were abducted for a week in a village called Sasira in Burundi on the other side of the Rusizi river. She was given to one of the soldiers as his "wife" and lived under a temporary shelter made from a sheet of plastic.[121]

In October 2001 a farmer from Sange told Human Rights Watch researchers that his wife had been raped only a few days earlier. Burundian rebels he believes to have been FNL forces attacked his house on October 26. There were four men, two of whom took him into the bush and threatened him, while two others took his wife to another place in the bush and raped her.[122]

Local people attributed a food shortage in Uvira in late 2001 in part to the refusal of women to go tend their fields outside Uvira, a refusal motivated by fear of rape and other kinds of attacks by soldiers and other combatants.

Sexual Violence in North Kivu
At the time of research for this report in late 2001, military activity was less intense in North Kivu than in South Kivu. Some soldiers and combatants nonetheless raped women and girls frequently. As in the south, RCD soldiers are established in the towns, like Goma, the major town of the region, but they control only limited parts of the countryside. Armed Hutu combatants dominate much of the territory of Masisi, Rutshuru, and Walikale, although the RPA, together with the RCD, launched a major effort to drive them from the region in 2001. Some of these Hutu combatants are part of ALIR, the best organized and largest of the Rwandan rebel units in Congo. Although ALIR commanders apparently ordered their forces not to harm civilians when a large number of

---

[121] Human Rights Watch group interview, Uvira, November 1, 2001. On abductions by Burundian rebel forces see also "Neglecting Justice in Making Peace," *A Human Rights Watch Report*, vol.12, No.2 (A), April 2000.

[122] Human Rights Watch interview, Uvira, October 31, 2001.

them crossed into Rwanda in May 2001, they seem not to have extended this order to Congolese territory.[123]

In March 2001, a group of Congolese were on their way to market in Kitchanga, Masisi territory, about sixty kilometers north of Goma. Innocente Y., a woman who was part of the group, said that they were suddenly attacked by "many, many, perhaps a hundred, Interahamwe." She said that she and the others were sure that the assailants were "Interahamwe," although they were in uniform. They were very dirty, meaning they had been living in the bush, and they spoke Kinyarwanda. They killed the two men who were accompanying the women, then picked eight women to carry off the goods they had been taking to market as loot. Her captors took Innocente Y. deeper into the bush where she was held for two days. Five men raped her repeatedly during this time. She risked her life by fleeing the camp. As she ran away, she saw the body of another woman who she believed had tried to flee and had been caught.[124]

Claire L. was attacked by an RCD soldier while gathering wood in an area near Goma in May 2000:

> I was going out to find wood for some construction. I was on the road and I was with my mother. My mother was helping me put wood on my head, when this soldier came and started yelling at us, saying: "You're Interahamwe—do you want to live or die?" He tied my mother to a banana tree, and he raped me. He was a RCD soldier. He had a grenade and a rifle and wore a uniform. He was one of the Tutsi soldiers who stayed in the hills above the town.[125]

Aloysie B., a widow with three children, was raped by "three Tutsi soldiers" in June 2000 as she was returning home from her bean field in Sake, some twenty-five kilometers from Goma. When she tried to resist, they cut her upper thigh with knives.[126]

Elise T., a twenty-nine-year-old widow, suffered a similar experience in the hands of Kinyarwanda-speaking RCD soldiers at the end of 1999. She was alone tending her beans in a field close to Sake in the middle of the morning. The

---

[123] "Observing the Rules of War?" *A Human Rights Watch Report*, vol.13, no.8 (A), December 2001.

[124] Human Rights Watch interview, Sake, October 26, 2001.

[125] Human Rights Watch interview, Goma, October 25, 2001.

[126] Human Rights Watch interview, Sake, October 26, 2001.

soldiers threatened her with death if she resisted, and each of the eight soldiers raped her, "one after the other." They then made her walk a long distance with them in order, she felt, to terrify her. She became pregnant as a result of the rape and, like so many others, did not consult a doctor after she was raped.[127]

Hélène C. was raped while working away from home in October 2001. An RCD soldier came looking for the owner of the house she was staying in. She was alone at that moment. He asked her for a glass of water and, as she went to get it, he grabbed her from behind. "He put his hand over my mouth. I fought back. He kicked me in the stomach and I fell over. It took less than ten minutes," she said. "he took his gun and left." She added,

> There was no blood, just some pain for a few days. I thought I was just a little injured. I didn't think I could identify him. They would just say [Hélène] did this and so I said nothing. I thought it would just pass.[128]

Commenting on responsibility for the attack, she said:

> I don't just blame the soldier who did this to me. I also blame the RCD. I think the war brought this to me. We [women] are victims of the war. We don't take up arms but we, the women, suffer the most.[129]

This was the second time she had been assaulted, although the first time, in 1997, she had managed to escape. That time a Rwandan army commander had tried to rape her. She said he was an "*Afande*"[130] in charge of the Mushaki military camp in North Kivu at the time. She told us: "[In trying to resist] I was stung by grasses—as though I was stung by bees. He chased me and fired two shots at me. I said to the Afande: 'Kill me if you have to—I can't do it.'"[131]

---

[127] Human Rights Watch interview, Sake, October 26, 2001.

[128] Human Rights Watch inteview, Goma, October 26, 2001.

[129] Human Rights Watch interview, Goma, October 26, 2001.

[130] "Afande" is a Kiswahili title used when speaking to soldiers, police etc. The term became associated particularly with members of the RPA when the RPA fought alongside the AFDL in the 1996/7 war. An "Afande," or "Afande," still generally refers to a soldier (usually high ranking) of Rwandan, RPA, and/or Tutsi origin.

[131] Human Rights Watch interview, Goma, October 26, 2001.

Twenty-year-old Antoinette E. was raped after school one day in early 2000 when she went to get water. An RCD soldier from the nearby military camp came down the hill from the camp toward her, offering to help carry the water, but then turned on her and raped her. When she resisted, he cut her shoulder with a knife, leaving a thick scar. She cried and went home but did not seek medical attention. She became pregnant as a result of the rape. At that time she lived with her family and went to school. As a result of the rape, the family rejected her and she had to leave school. She now has the sole care of the baby, who is handicapped, and survives by washing clothes or working as a laborer on other people's land. "The RCD soldiers do whatever they want," she said.[132]

Goma Town

Although the RCD has a stronger grip over Goma than over any other city in eastern Congo, there is a high degree of insecurity in the city, including rapes, armed robberies, and attacks on residents. In some cases perpetrators have been RCD or RPA soldiers, in others Congolese policemen. RCD authorities have acknowledged that officials have been involved in some of these crimes. According to Agence France Press, they issued a statement read on the radio which said: "These reprehensible acts are often committed with the complicity of certain elements closely tied to political or military authorities and by errant soldiers."[133] Some of the attackers may also be members of predominantly Hutu armed groups or deserters from such groups or from the army.

Twenty-one-year-old Delphine W. was raped during an armed robbery in Goma by three Rwandan and Congolese soldiers in September 2001:

> I don't know what time it was, I was asleep. Four men, soldiers, came to see what they wanted to steal. They were armed with knives. They spoke Kinyarwanda and Kiswahili— the two languages of the military. Some were Rwandan and some Congolese. Some were in civilian clothing and some in military uniform. I didn't see their faces. They chose our house by chance; there are lots of other houses in the neighborhood. There was just me and my mother in the house. They forced the door open.

---

[132] Human Rights Watch interview, Sake, October 26, 2001.

[133] Agence France Press, "Rwanda-backed rebels retake town in east DR Congo: rebels," Kigali, November 10, 2001.

I was in bed. When the door opened I cried out. They said they needed the girl. Three of the men raped me. They did not rape my mother. They said they didn't need the mother, just the girl. They asked if I was married and I said no. They asked me if I had ever been taken by a man and why. [One of the men] said what girl has never been taken by men? It was the first time I had ever slept with men. They said if I refused, they'd kill me. The first one who took me hit me with his hands; he took me by force. I asked for mercy. He said that if I didn't let him do it he would kill me. I refused. He hit me so I accepted. I was still in bed. The others didn't hit me. The second one wanted to put his thing in my mouth—I refused. The three raped me, the fourth left. When they took me, I felt sick.

In the night I cried and said to God: "Why did you want it to be like that? I refused so many men. Then I had to accept men I had never met before, I didn't even know their faces."

My mother told me I should thank God I was still alive. She told me to be brave and not say anything to other families so as not to lose my reputation. She said if I publicize it, I might not get a husband. They could say I have illnesses because I was with soldiers.

I was sick for three days. I felt cold. It felt as if they had put chili in me—it burned. There was lots of blood running out. I bled for five days, as if I was having a period. I haven't had a normal period yet [the rape had taken place about five weeks before]. I was in pain afterwards but that is all right now. In the morning my mother gave me water to wash with, just water. I haven't seen a doctor or a nurse. I don't have enough money to have tests—I have problems finding money for my studies, I can't afford medical things too. For my exams, we had to pay each teacher, one dollar, one dollar....I didn't have enough for that either.

I sometimes get headaches and feel dizzy and can't do anything. I sometimes can't breathe and feel as if I am going to die. This has happened three times since it happened, it never happened before. I go to pray but that doesn't seem to

help. At times I feel out of my body. It happened four times
and then goes—then I feel alive again.

I spoke to my mother about it—she says I must not feel sorry
about it because I am still alive. The neighbors don't know—
my mother told them they didn't do anything, just stole.[134]

Extraordinary Brutality

Assailants who raped women and girls frequently beat, whipped, or
otherwise physically abused them before, during, and after the crime. Those who
abducted women and girls for weeks or months mistreated them regularly in
addition to raping them. Rapists also insulted and humiliated their victims.

Beyond such usual kinds of abuse, there were other cases where the rapists
inflicted severe injury on their victims by penetrating their vaginas with sticks or
other objects or by mutilating their sexual organs with such weapons as knives
or razor blades. A gynecologist said that in his many years of work he had never
seen atrocities like those committed against women who had been raped whom
he has treated recently. Among the cases are women whose clitoris and vagina
lips had been cut off with razor blades. He said that one of his patients explained
this by saying, "It is just hatred."[135] The father of four daughters, the doctor
commented, "I have the feeling that if you are born a woman in this country,
you are condemned to death at birth....Why are we silent about this?"[136]

Uniformed, armed soldiers identified by witnesses as "Banyamulenge"
surrounded a group of women working in a field in Kigongo, about ten
kilometers south of Uvira in July 2001. Most of the women managed to run and
hide, including the woman who informed us about the incident. However she
saw the attackers grab a Burundian woman she described as Hutu. The attackers
accused the woman of being the wife of the Mai-Mai, according to the woman
who watched from her hiding place. The captive woman denied this, claiming
that she had come to seek refuge in Congo from Burundi. Seven soldiers took
the Burundian woman off and raped her. Then one of the rapists put a gun into
her vagina and shot her. The assailants then left. The witness and other women
came out of their hiding place and tried to take the badly injured women for

---

[134] Human Rights Watch interview, Goma, October 25, 2001. Many people told our
researchers that families of women and girls raped during armed robberies frequently
claimed—without being believed—that no rape happened. Several rape survivors in
addition to Delphine admitted to having made such false denials.

[135] Human Rights Watch interview, Bukavu, October 17, 2001.

[136] Ibid.

medical assistance, but she died on the way. The following morning, the same attackers returned and threatened to kill the other women. According to the witness, there had been two other similar cases in Kabumbe recently. In each RCD soldiers shot women whom they had raped in the vagina, killing them. The witness, a forty-year-old widow, has not gone back to the fields since seeing the Burundian woman killed.[137]

On June 1, 2000 an RCD soldier raped a twenty-five-year-old woman on near Nundu in Fizi territory. He then shot her three times in her genitals. Miraculously she did not die. She was in hospital for several months and needs further operations and treatment.[138] According to local sources of information, there has been no official investigation of this crime.

In some cases, rapists react with extraordinary cruelty to any efforts to resist their assault. One mother described the treatment of her daughter, Monique B., aged twenty, who was engaged to be married:

> On May 15 of this year [2001], four heavily armed combatants—they were Hutu—came to our house at 9 p.m. Everyone in the neighborhood had fled. I wanted to hide my children, but I didn't have time. They took my husband and tied him to a pole in the house. My four-month-old baby started crying and I started breastfeeding him and then they left me alone.
>
> They went after my daughter, and I knew they would rape her. But she resisted and said she would rather die than have relations with them. They cut off her left breast and put it in her hand. They said, "Are you still resisting us?" She said she would rather die than be with them. They cut off her genital labia and showed them to her. She said, "Please kill me." They took a knife and put it to her neck and then made a long vertical incision down her chest and split her body open. She was crying but finally she died. She died with her breast in her hand.

---

[137] Human Rights Watch interview, Uvira, November 1, 2001.

[138] See Héritiers de la Justice, "Situation des Droits de l'Homme en République Démocratique du Congo (RDC) cas du Sud-Kivu. Une population désesperée, délassée et prise en otage," Rapport Avril-Décembre 2000 for reports of other rape cases committed by RCD troops and rebel groups opposed to the RCD including the FDD.

RCD officers came and looked at the body. But then they went away and I don't think they ever did anything about it. I didn't talk to other authorities because I thought it was a military matter. There is no electricity there, and we couldn't see much, but we could hear her scream and see what happened when we saw the body in the morning. I never saw the attackers again, but I couldn't even see them well that night. They didn't stay after they killed my daughter.[139]

Children and the Elderly

Some rapists attacked the young and very young, betraying the usually acknowledged obligation of the adult to protect the child. They may have wanted to avoid exposure to HIV/AIDS by raping those who had had no previous sex partners. Some Congolese interviewed also said that there is a belief that sex with a young child could eliminate the virus.

An unidentified assailant or assailants, apparently in uniform, raped a five-year-old child in Goma in late 2001. When later taken to the hospital, the child had lost so much blood that she needed a transfusion. The mother of the victim related the case to us and told us that it was some time before she could begin to walk normally again.[140]

In areas of military activity, soldiers and armed combatants raped young girls as they did adult women, to help establish their dominance in the region. In May 2001 a fourteen-year-old girl went to the forest near the Kahuzi-Biega National Park because she hoped to start earning some money like older girls and women by trading in charcoal. She and some ten others were returning home with their loads of charcoal when armed combatants, whom she identified as Interahamwe, came upon them. She and another girl, aged sixteen, were abducted by two combatants who kept them in the forest for three days. She said, "At first we resisted, but they kept hitting us. We finally gave in and they raped us."[141] After three days the combatants left and the girls found their way home.

At about the same period, another fourteen-year-old and two older girls were also attacked in the same region when they were coming back from the forest shortly after dark. Three combatants abducted them and made them walk

---

[139] Human Rights Watch interview, Murhesa, October 19, 2001.

[140] Human Rights Watch interview, Goma, October 25, 2001.

[141] Human Rights Watch interview, Murhesa, October 19, 2001.

until about 2 a.m. deeper into the forest. Each girl had to stay with one combatant and to have sex with him. The abductors kept them there for five days and made them obey by threatening to shoot them.[142]

In Walungu, near the Kahuzi-Bienga National Park, armed soldiers attacked a home in April 2000 and killed the parents of the family. The six daughters fled but returned home two weeks later. Because they were so afraid they slept together in a single bed. One of the sisters described a second attack on their home:

> The soldiers came again. It was about 10 p.m. There were eight of them; I never saw them all together but I think there were that many. They shined a flashlight in our faces and threw us on the ground. They raped all of us twice rapidly, one by one. Our neighbors didn't help us; maybe they didn't hear us all crying. The soldiers didn't stay long after that. They seemed to be afraid too.

The youngest of the sisters was nine years old and the others were thirteen, fifteen, seventeen, nineteen and twenty. The girls believed that boys from the village, perhaps themselves fifteen or sixteen years old, joined the soldiers in raping them. The oldest sister said:

> After we were raped, we went to a manioc field until 1 a.m. We didn't tell anyone what happened but we found that what happened was already spread all around the neighborhood— everyone knew. And everywhere we went, people talked about those girls who were raped. The neighbors were afraid the same thing would happen in their families.
>
> I can't go back to that village as long as people know and remember all this. I'm trying not to be too preoccupied but just to concentrate on my studies. I don't ever want to see people of that neighborhood again.[143]

The girls are now staying with the family and friends of a priest in another community except for the oldest who, with the encouragement of the priest, recently passed an examination to enter university.

---

[142] Human Rights Watch interview, Murhesa, October 19, 2001.

[143] Human Rights Watch interview, Bukavu, October 18, 2001.

On October 19, 2001, armed FDD combatants raped two children in a village near Baraka on Lake Tanganyika. Their mother, Agnès T., told Human Rights Watch researchers that the assailants raped her thirteen-year-old daughter and her sixteen-year-old son in front of her. FDD rebels had attacked a group of fishermen, including her son. They tied them up and later that night brought the tied-up boy to her home in search of money. Agnès T.'s husband managed to escape through a window but the assailants caught her and tied her up. Four rebels raped her daughter. They also raped her son, "like a girl," said Agnès T. Then the combatants looted the house and left. Both children suffered infections as a result, and the girl spent a month in the hospital.[144]

Thirteen-year-old Thérèse K. was raped by RCD soldiers who attacked her home in the town of Uvira. Her grandmother, with whom she lives, managed to flee but left her behind. Seven men in uniforms and armed with guns who spoke Kinyarwanda—Banyamulenge, she claimed—broke into the house. One raped her.[145]

Juliette M., then fifteen years old, was raped by RPA soldiers in Kabare town, about ten kilometers from Bukavu. She was on her way to visit her grandparent to get a chicken for Christmas in 1998. Near a military camp in Kabare, she saw lots of soldiers, one of whom asked her to fetch him a mug. She did so, she said, because he was a soldier and she felt she had to respect him. He told her he knew she loved him, which she denied, and then he threatened to rape her. He called four other men and they took her to a small house in the military camp. They told her: "If you don't want to...we'll hit you." They undressed her and each of the four raped her. Then they chased her away. She went home crying but found support from her mother who took her to a local health center. Juliette M. said that she never wants to see a man again. Because of what happened to her, she says: "I can't marry. But I can study and one day help children."[146]

Twelve-year-old Eléonore R. was staying with her aunt and uncle in Goma when unidentified armed attackers broke in to their house in August 2001. They used a common method known as "katarina"—throwing large rocks at the lock on the door until it breaks. She said:

---

[144] Human Rights Watch interview, Uvira, October 31, 2001. This is the only case of male rape reported to Human Rights Watch researchers. Because rape is considered even more shameful for a male victim, crimes of this kind are less likely to be reported than those involving female victims.

[145] Human Rights Watch interview, Uvira, November 3, 2001.

[146] Human Rights Watch interview, Bukavu, October 19, 2001.

They used two stones to get in. Four [men] came into the house and there were more outside. They opened the door, took the papa, tied him up, hit the mama, and took everything in the house. They made a lot of noise. I hid under the bed.

They then came to my room. One was very tall, the other fat. I didn't know them and didn't really see them. They had guns and flashlights. They spoke Kinyarwanda and Kiswahili. When I refused one hit me twice with his hand. Then he did the act. There were four other children in the room, all younger. The man who did it told the others to close their eyes. I also closed my eyes. They stopped when the blood came.

I think they attacked only our house that night. They might have gone to other houses but I didn't hear of it. Afterwards lots of people from the neighborhood came.

In the morning I went to the clinic to see a nurse. I was torn and there was lots of blood. I was given a transfusion, pills, and an injection. I think they were vitamins. I was bleeding a lot. I don't have any pain now and feel fine though sometimes my legs seem to become paralyzed. I didn't have any other tests. The other mothers in the neighborhood helped me, gave me things.[147]

In another case, six armed and masked men in uniform broke into a home in Bukavu and attacked the father of the family with machetes. Two men took the mother away while the others raped the fifteen-year-old daughter for an hour. When she started to cry, they put the barrel of a gun in her mouth. She was severely beaten and suffered both internal and external injuries.[148]

In some cases, young girls were raped by men in positions of authority or related to those in positions of authority. Fifteen-year-old Grace C. was abducted after school in Goma on October 15, 2001 and held captive for eight days by an official in the RCD administration, a man she had seen once or twice at a neighbor's house. Although a civilian, the abductor was sufficiently important to have an armed military escort. Grace's mother spent days trying to

---

[147] Human Rights Watch interview, Goma, October 25, 2001.

[148] Human Rights Watch interview, Bukavu, October 20, 2001.

trace her daughter. She paid several hundred dollars in transport and telephone expenses for RCD security officers and soldiers to locate her daughter. She believes that at least some of them knew where her daughter was and who was holding her. When they failed to help her, she went to see an adviser of Bizima Karaha, Head of Security and Intelligence. He, she said, reacted immediately and angrily, ordering that the girl be produced within two hours. Although Grace's mother still had to pay for the transport costs of those sent to get her, her daughter was brought home immediately.

During the eight days she was held, Grace C. was raped several times and threatened at gun point. She asked several times to be taken home. She was forced, on two occasions (once with a revolver at her throat), to phone her mother and lie about her whereabouts. On another occasion, she was forced to ask her mother to accept a delegation sent to arrange her marriage to her captor. The man who raped her claimed he wanted to marry her and ordered her to tell others that she wanted to live with him.[149] Judicial authorities investigated this case and detained the alleged perpetrator for several days. He was subsequently released and the case has not been brought to court.[150]

In another case the son of a local official raped an eleven-year-old girl at a village not far from Goma. He caught the child when she had gone with another girl to gather manioc leaves in the fields. He tied up the other girl and raped the eleven-year-old. She suffered a fistula from the rape and for some time evacuated her feces through her vagina. The child's family reported the rape to local officials. The rapist supposedly paid some compensation to an official, who failed to pass any of it on to the victim or her family. The rapist left the area and was not prosecuted.[151]

Assailants also raped and otherwise abused elderly women, normally persons entitled to great respect in local society. In October 2000 a large number of Mai-Mai found a great-grandmother who had taken refuge in the forest with her grandson and his family. The Mai-Mai apparently knew that her grandson had worked in a local government office and so accused him of collaborating with the RCD. She said:

> About one year ago, we were living in the forest. I was with
> my grandson and his baby boy who was just born. A large

---

[149] Human Rights Watch interview, Goma, October 27, 2001.

[150] Electronic communication from family member to Human Rights Watch, December 2001; Human Rights Watch telephone interview, December 2001.

[151] Human Rights Watch interview, Sake, October 26, 2001.

number of Mai-Mai attacked us. The baby was with me and they threw him down. They beat my grandson with a pounding stick [the kind used to pound dried manioc into flour] until his brains and his eyes spilled out of his head.

Then they raped me. They put a knife to each of my eyes, and they said that if I cried, they would cut my eyes out. There were many of them when they raped me, but I don't know how many. They were filthy. They wore masks and animal skins. They said they would save everyone, but only if we all obeyed them.[152]

Forced Labor

Combatants abducted women and girls and held them for periods up to a year and a half, forcing them during that time to provide both sexual services and gender-specific work. In addition to being raped, women and girls were obliged to do domestic labor, such as finding and transport firewood and water, gathering and preparing food, and doing laundry for the men who held them captive. For example, the young women abducted by Hutu armed men from villages near the Kahuzi-Biega forest told our team that they were forced to work for their captors. Béatrice K., Cécile K., and Valérie J., who were captives together—their cases are cited above—had to fetch water and to cook for the three men who held them in the forest.[153] Cécile K. said: "Sometimes we refused to cook and eat because afterwards they always wanted sex."[154] When Valérie J. refused to cook, one man got angry and slapped her.[155]

When combatants moved camp, they forced the women and girls under their control to transport their belongings. When they raided to seize goods, they obliged the women and girls to carry their loot to their bases.[156] Sixteen-year-old Véronique K. from a village in Katana territory, near the Kahuzi-Biega forest, was abducted by Hutu armed men in September 2001. She and a neighbor's girl had to carry the loot to the forest. When she was released after a week of sexual abuse, one of the combatants said to her: "Go back to the village, earn dollars,

---

[152] Human Rights Watch interview, Shabunda, October 22, 2001.

[153] Human Rights Watch interviews, Bukavu and Murhesa, October 18 and 19, 2001.

[154] Human Rights Watch interview, Murhesa, October 19, 2001.

[155] Human Rights Watch interview, Murhesa, October 19, 2001.

[156] Human Rights Watch interviews, Murhesa, October 19, 2001.

and afterwards we will come back and get you again."[157] When Innocente Y. was abducted by Hutu rebels near Kitchanga in North Kivu—her case is cited above—she and several other women had to carry the goods they were going to sell on the market to the forest instead, providing their captors with fresh food.

In one case, combatants forced female captives to accompany them on a raid to help in abducting other women, a plan which failed because the targeted village had been abandoned.[158] In another case, described below, women with training as nurses sometimes provided rudimentary medical care for the injured.

The captors ordinarily held the women and girls at places distant from their homes and often in areas that were unfamiliar to them, making it difficult for them to try to escape. In some cases, women and girls were kept under armed guard.

Women and girls held in the forest ordinarily lived in conditions of misery in temporary shelters constructed of leaves, wood, and sheets of plastic. In one case captors deprived the women of sleeping mats and forced them to sleep on the ground. In some cases, women and girls had no shelter and were exposed to drenching rains whenever the weather was bad. Often short of water and with no soap, women found it difficult to stay clean. In some cases, their efforts at cleanliness were frustrated by having to associate with captors who never washed and were infested with fleas. Some Mai-Mai apparently believe that washing their bodies will diminish their strength and so do not bathe even if water is available.

Captors sometimes released their female captives because they were attacked or feared they might be attacked by the opposing side. In other cases, the captors released the women and girls because they planned to abduct others, apparently wishing to ensure a regular supply of women not exhausted or made ill by the rigors of life in the bush. In several cases, the captors informed women and girls whom they released that they would be back to take them another time. In at least one case documented by Human Rights Watch, captors who had raped a woman and held her for some time allowed her to return to the place in the

---

[157] Human Rights Watch interview, Bukavu, October 19, 2001.

[158] Human Rights Watch interview, Bukavu, October 18, 2001.

forest where she had previously lived; over the next months they returned occasionally to require her to come and provide them with service on a short-term basis.

THE AFTERMATH OF RAPE AND OTHER
FORMS OF SEXUAL VIOLENCE

Stigmatization of Victims

Women and girls who have been raped and otherwise sexually abused have been psychologically damaged as well as physically injured by these crimes, and many will never fully recover. A significant number of women and girls have become pregnant as a result of being raped and an unknown number have been infected with HIV, dramatically altering their future lives, livelihoods, and prospects. Other family and community members may also be psychologically or physically affected as a result of sexual violence against women and girls. A woman abducted and raped by Kinyarwanda-speaking attackers said simply that afterwards "my head was not right."[159]

The situation of rape victims is made worse by the stigma that is attached to such violence. In many cases these women and girls are ostracized, and find themselves at the margins of society.

One doctor treated a fifteen-year-old girl who had been raped by several men as an outpatient to avoid drawing attention to her case. He also treated her without charge. He commented, "We can do little else to prevent her being rejected. It's not her fault," he said. "Physically she'll probably get better, although we don't know yet if she contracted any other illness. And on the psychological level, it remains a problem. She lost her virginity, which is something very important in the village. She can't even talk about it."[160]

In some cases husbands rejected their wives upon learning they had been raped, sometimes on the pretext that the woman must have consented to the sexual relations. In one such case, a woman raped by RCD soldiers said:

> Afterwards I went home. I tried to hide it from my husband but he found out. He said that I had accepted it voluntarily. He said this although I had bruises and marks where the soldiers had pressed their fingernails into my inner thigh.[161]

In another case, a woman who had been raped by a former Rwandan soldier hoped to keep the crime from her husband but sought advice from her pastor:

---

[159] Human Rights Watch interview, Bukavu, October 18, 2001.

[160] Human Rights Watch interview, Bukavu, October, 2001.

[161] Human Rights Watch interview, Uvira, October 31, 2001

64

When I got home, I went to the pastor to tell him what had happened. His wife heard our conversation, and she went around and told everyone about it. Now I am an outcast. No one will come to see me or share anything with me. My second husband said he was unlucky with wives because he had already lost two wives before me. We don't get along. Sometimes he says I should go back to [my first] husband...or I should go be with another man in the forest.[162]

Some husbands simply put their wives out the door, refusing further contact with them. In others they allowed the women to remain in the household but took a second wife, relegating the rape victim to a subordinate position.[163]

Families of husbands and of the victims themselves sometimes rejected women and girls who had been raped. Francine M., a thirty-five year old widow and mother of six, was raped by three RPA soldiers at Kasika, South Kivu, in August 1998. They also killed her husband in front of her. Afterwards her husband's brothers accused her of being a "traitor," an "accomplice" of the attackers, suggesting she could not have survived otherwise. They said she had become "everyone's woman." She left Kasika and is now living in Bukavu. She continues to suffer from abdominal pain three years later. "My body has become sad," she said. "I have no happiness."[164]

Husbands and families often weighed many issues in determining their response to the rape of a woman in the household. In deciding the long-term results of the crime, they considered whether the woman might have become pregnant and if so what responsibilities would be involved in raising the child. Families also considered the possibility that the victim might have been infected, particularly by HIV/AIDS, which would impose the burden of care on the family. The amount of public attention given to the crime also influenced the reaction of husbands or others in the family. This is one reason why victims preferred keeping silent about the crimes.

Women and girls rejected by husbands and families were often impoverished as well as humiliated. Francine M., who moved to Bukavu with her six children, now sells avocados and rents a house for three dollars a month, an amount she has difficulty paying.[165] Another young woman who had been

---

[162] Human Rights Watch interview, Goma, October 25, 2001.

[163] Human Rights Watch interview, Bukavu, October 16, 2001.

[164] Human Rights Watch interview, Bukavu, October 18, 2001.

[165] Human Rights Watch interview, Bukavu, October 18, 2001.

raped by Hutu combatants in Masisi was rejected by her husband. Now in Goma, she is pregnant and has no permanent roof over her head. She lives in the ruins of destroyed houses and earns small sums of money by transporting heavy loads.[166] Several girls we interviewed at Sake, near Goma, had been expelled from their homes after they were raped at a young age. Some of them were pregnant. They were often forced into hazardous and low-paying labor. For example some of the women interviewed earned money by carrying heavy loads or working as household help.[167]

Unmarried women and girls who became pregnant as a result of rape were far less likely to find husbands in the future and so risked remaining always on the margins of society. In the estimation of one doctor, an unmarried woman who had a child in such circumstances would have only a 20 percent chance of being married in the future. [168]According to one group of Congolese women, a girl who had been raped and given birth was "a girl no boy can marry."[169] Yet most unmarried girls who became pregnant as a result of rape generally gave birth to the children even though they understood that doing so made it impossible to hide the rape and also entailed the burdens of bringing up the child. Congo is a predominantly Roman Catholic country and abortion is illegal under Congolese law and not condoned by Congolese culture, even in the case of rape.[170] According to one doctor, women and girls who decided to end pregnancies sought abortions not from medical doctors but from unqualified personnel, with all the attendant risks of complications. "If it is done," he said, "it's done by charlatans."[171]

One young woman recounted what happened after she was raped by an RCD soldier in October 2001. At first she said nothing to anyone else but she finally confided in her employer, who gave her the money for a pregnancy test and HIV test. When she learned that she was pregnant, the employers suggested she have an abortion. "I spoke with my father," said the young woman, "and he asked me—would a child stop you continuing with your studies? I said no and

---

[166] Human Rights Watch inteview, Goma, August 1, 2001.

[167] Human Rights Watch interviews in Sake, October 26, 2001.

[168] Human Rights Watch interview, Bukavu, 17, 2001.

[169] Human Rights Watch group interview with Banyamulenge women, Bukavu, October 18, 2001.

[170] Under arts. 165 and 166 of the Congolese penal code, abortion is prohibited and anyone assisting a woman to have an abortion can be punished.

[171] Human Rights Watch interview, Bukavu, 17, 2001.

he said I should keep the child. My father is a Christian. He said he would stand by me." She continued:

> I haven't yet told my brothers. I don't know how I am going to tell them. I don't know what I am going to say, how I am going to introduce it. I already don't know how to explain why I vomit. I stay in my room all day. If God gives me this child and the child asks who his father is, what am I supposed to say?[172]

Some husbands have supported their wives after they have been raped. One woman raped by Mai-Mai and FDD combatants near Kazimia in June 2001 needed three days of hospital care to begin her recovery. When she returned home, her husband, a development worker, welcomed her. He said, "We are together—it [the rape] was not her fault."[173]

A greater willingness to speak out about the crimes has helped reduce the stigmatization from which the survivors suffered. In Shabunda, where women and girls have been the most outspoken about having been raped, they have formed an association of 500 members to support women and girls who have been raped.

In other areas, priests are using their sermons to publicize the availability of medical treatment and counseling for victims of sexual violence at church funded centers in Bukavu. Although few will be able to avail themselves of these services, simply raising the issue of sexual violence publicly in such a forum helps reduce the stigma attached to sexually abused women and girls and makes it easier for them to seek help.

Medical Consequences and HIV/AIDS

Many women and girls suffer from injuries, internal bleeding, fistulas and incontinence as a result of rape. Some are pregnant and experience medical complications during the pregnancy. Many women and girls also contract sexually transmitted diseases, including HIV/AIDS. Experts estimate that about 60 percent of regular troops and militia-men in Congo are infected with HIV/AIDS and have warned that the war exacerbates an existing HIV/AIDS crisis. The people in Congo have yet to realize the full extent of the destruction brought upon them by the sexual violence used against women and girls.

---

[172] Human Rights Watch interview, Goma, October 26, 2001.

[173] Human Rights Watch group interview, Uvira, November 2, 2001.

Few women or girls seek medical treatment after rape because health care and testing for sexually transmitted diseases or HIV/AIDS is so expensive, because in some areas there are few health care service providers and most of them are men, and because seeking care makes it likely that the rape will become known and the victim will be stigmatized. Generally, medical staff are poorly trained, have little or no specialized experience in treating the consequences of sexual violence, are not paid, and are demoralized; medical centers are poorly equipped; and many facilities have been pillaged or destroyed.

One doctor said, "Those we see are just a sample. We probably see only the extreme cases."[174] A nurse agreed. "If [women and girls] have been raped and are really sick and they have to seek medical attention, some go to hospitals," she said. "If they don't have to, they don't speak about it to anyone, and don't seek medical help."[175] Some women and girls have been seriously and sometimes permanently injured or disabled in the course of being raped or otherwise sexually assaulted. Women and girls who have survived acts such as being shot in the vagina, as described above, or repeated gang rape, amateur emergency surgery, and so on are likely to have very serious clinical problems.

In one particularly serious case, a woman who had recently given birth was gang-raped by four Kiswahili-speaking armed men in the forest near Shabunda. A fistula developed between her vagina and her rectum. Unable to leave the forest all she could do was washed herself with warm water and leaves from the trees. She related:

> After a month I went to the nurses in the bush. These were nurses who had been taken hostage by the Mai-Mai. The nurses tried to stitch me up, using the kind of cord that is used to braid hair. There was no anesthetic and no hygiene. But it came apart after some days.[176]

Fifteen months later this young woman reached Shabunda and was finally been able to seek medical assistance. She is hoping to go to Bukavu for specialized surgery to repair the fistula. Many doctors do not have the facilities or expertise to treat such patients, even if the women and girls can reach them in

---

[174] Human Rights Watch interview, October, 2001. Because doctors have been arrested or threatened after speaking with journalists, we omit the names and places of work of doctors interviewed for this report.

[175] Human Rights Watch interview, Bukavu, October 16, 2001.

[176] Human Rights Watch interview, Shabunda, October 22, 2001.

the first place. Even with the best possible treatment, many of these women and girls are disabled for life and need long-term therapy. The psychological trauma caused by rape is likewise rarely addressed, and the reluctance to discuss the experience even with family members or friends compounds the problem.

A significant number of women and girls are infected with sexually transmitted diseases through rape and for any or all of the above reasons do not seek treatment unless it is absolutely necessary. The large majority of rape victims interviewed had never received any medical treatment after the rape, and often did not even tell doctors about the rape when they gave birth. Social workers and medical staff confirmed that only a small minority of victims ever get any treatment. Thus, many relatively easily treatable sexually transmitted diseases remain untreated, some causing considerable pain and inconvenience to the woman, and some causing irreversible consequences. The most deadly disease that can be contracted through rape is HIV/AIDS. Not only are the lives of HIV-positive women and girls shortened and their livelihood possibilities seriously impaired, but being HIV-positive or even being suspected of being positive adds to the stigma of rape to make for a double stigmatization of these women and girls. One woman who had been raped said that her husband rejected her, saying he was afraid that she had contracted HIV and would "contaminate" him.[177] The scarcity and high cost of HIV testing makes it more difficult for women who are not infected to demonstrate this to their husbands and families.

In Resolution 1308 (2000), the Security Council explicitly recognized that the HIV/AIDS pandemic is exacerbated by armed conflict, as have others.[178] The secretary-general reported to the General Assembly in 2000 on children in armed conflict and noted the "...haunting images, from place after place, of adolescent victims of rape, which has become as much a weapon of warfare as bullets and machetes...Armed conflicts also increasingly serve as vectors for the HIV/AIDS pandemic, which follows closely on the heels of armed troops and in the corridors of conflict."[179] It has been reported that rates of sexually

---

[177] Human Rights Watch interview, Sake, October 26, 2001.

[178] United Nations Security Council Resolution 1308 (untitled), July 17, 2000. See also Graça Machel, "The Impact of Armed Conflict on Children: A critical review of progress made by and obstacles encountered in increasing protection for war-affected children," report prepared for and presented at the International Conference on War-Affected Children, September 2000, Winnipeg, Canada, p.12, located at http://www.waraffectedchildren.gc.ca/machel-e.asp, accessed May 23, 2002).

[179] Report of the Secretary-General to the Security Council on Children in Armed Conflict, pursuant to Security Council resolution 1261 (1999), Para 3. A/55/163-S/2000/712

transmitted diseases among soldiers are two to five times higher than those of civilian populations and that during armed conflict the rate of infection can be up to fifty times higher.[180] The U.S. Institute for Peace in 2001 estimated that the HIV prevalence rate among combatants in the D.R. Congo war is 60 percent.[181] It is likely that a high percentage of Rwandan soldiers are HIV-positive.[182] Dr. Tshioko Kweteminga of WHO-Congo has commented that the displacement and multiple troop movements between Congo and neighboring countries have set Congo up for a major "explosion of HIV/AIDS," a view held by many.[183] Rwandan troops returning with the virus from Congo will put the civilian population of Rwanda at increased risk of contracting HIV.

The national HIV prevalence rate in Congo was officially given as 5.1 percent as of end 1999—derived from sentinel site data[184]—but this figure is widely thought to underestimate the current prevalence.[185] In July 2001, WHO reported that national figures collected through the health information system cite just under 10,000 new cases of HIV for 2000. It commented, "But public health authorities estimate the real figures, based on the sentinel site information, are more like 173,000 new cases a year, with a total of almost 1.3 million adults and children already living with HIV."[186] Various surveys of

---

[180] Machel, "The Impact of Armed Conflict on Children," p.12.

[181] United States Institute for Peace, "Special Report: AIDS and Violent Conflict in Africa," October 2001, p.5. Also available at www.usip.org. (accessed May 23, 2002).

[182] In November 2001 the Rwandan newspaper *New Times* reported that "research made between 1997 and 2000 indicates that 4 percent of the Rwandan army are HIV positive, compared to the nation's average of 11.1 percent." This figure is unrealistically low. The report states that 56 percent of the RPA (presumably meaning those interviewed) had had sex without a condom. This would suggest that 44 percent have either never had sex or always use a condom, which would be a highly unlikely situation. "4 percent of RPA are HIV positive - Doctor," The New Times, November 5th - 7th, 2001, p.4.

[183] Quoted in World Health Organization, Democratic Republic of Congo Health Update, July 2001, p. 2. A delegation of British Parliamentarians recently expressed the same concern after a visit to eastern Congo. See *The Monitor*, "Defence Force Spreads HIV/AIDS - UK MPs", December 5, 2001.

[184] Sentinel site data are data from periodic surveys from a selection of representative locations.

[185] Joint United Nations Programme on HIV/AIDS and World Health Organization. Democratic Republic of the Congo – Epidemiological fact sheet on HIV/AIDS and sexually transmitted infections: Update.   Geneva, 2000. See also World Health Organization, Democratic Republic of Congo Health Update, July 2001, p. 2.

[186] World Health Organization, Democratic Republic of Congo Health Update, July 2001, p. 2.

women and girls in antenatal clinics in some of the bigger cities were conducted from the mid-1980s to the mid-1990s, but since then political instability and war have impeded regular surveillance. Eastern Congo is particularly devoid of good data.

Surveys in the last few years indicate that HIV prevalence among blood donors in the city of Bukavu is 10 to 12 percent, but it is not clear how representative this group is of the general population or of communities most affected by the war.[187] One NGO-based health expert estimated the prevalence in Bukavu to be of the order of 15 to 20 percent, given the results of various small-scale studies.[188] Prudence Shamavu, director of the Bukavu office of Fondation Femmes Plus, a national organization working against HIV/AIDS, said one study indicated that the HIV prevalence among prostitutes in the city of Bukavu is as high as 45 percent.[189] WHO reported that a study of patients in the General Hospital of Bukavu found a HIV infection rate of 32 percent among adult males, 54 percent among adult females, and 26.5 percent among children.[190] Health experts interviewed agreed that the prevalence of HIV/AIDS is growing rapidly in North and South Kivu and constitutes an urgent problem. They urged international assistance for conducting a valid prevalence survey.

Compared to other parts of eastern, central, and southern Africa, even those that are poorly served by health services, eastern Congo is desperately lacking in services related to HIV/AIDS. Services meant to prevent HIV/AIDS are almost nonexistent. The public health promotional messages and information campaigns that have come to be fairly widespread through much of Africa are virtually absent in eastern Congo. Shamavu noted it has been difficult to interest donors in usual preventive activities such as mass media campaigns, and donor funding is necessary as the authorities in the region have not allocated significant resources to HIV/AIDS programs.[191] She also noted that it has taken some time for all the relevant players in the health sector, including the Roman Catholic church, a major health service provider, to come to a consensus on the content of messages to disseminate.

---

[187] Human Rights Watch interview with Maria Masson, administrator of the Bureau des Oeuvres Medicales of the Roman Catholic Diocese of Bukavu, October 15, 2001.

[188] Human Rights Watch interview in Bukavu, October 17, 2001.

[189] Human Rights Watch interview in Bukavu, October 18, 2001.

[190] World Health Organization, Democratic Republic of Congo Health Update, July 2001, p. 2.

[191] Human Rights Watch interview in Bukavu, October 18, 2001.

Other services, notably access to HIV testing and counseling, are accessible only to a tiny percentage of the population through a few of the better equipped health facilities. HIV tests cost up to US $5 in some parts of the region, a price beyond the reach of much of the population. The majority of the women and girls met by Human Rights Watch researchers were aware of the possibility of HIV infection, and many indicated that if testing were accessible to them they would be tested. "Some women do ask for HIV tests and they want to know if they have sexually transmitted diseases. They dance when they find out that they're HIV-negative," said a health worker.[192] Antiretroviral treatment for HIV-positive women and girls or treatment to prevent mother-to-child transmission is virtually nonexistent. Even opportunistic infections, such as tuberculosis, diarrhea, meningitis and pneumonia, are mostly not treated because people cannot afford to pay for medicine.

The international organization Population Services International recently began a condom promotion campaign in Bukavu, but condoms have otherwise been and remain difficult to obtain. Médecins sans Frontières-Holland has begun a pilot activity in Bukavu providing information and counseling about sexual practices to young people, street children, and prostitutes.[193]

In agreement with considerable social science research, the U.N. Development Fund for Women (UNIFEM) claims that the HIV/AIDS epidemic "would not have reached such vast proportions" if women and girls in Africa and elsewhere had been able to refuse unwanted and unprotected sex.[194] A report to the U.N. Commission on the Status of Women concluded: "Women's and girls' relative lack of power over their bodies and their sex lives, which is supported and reinforced by their social and economic inequality, makes them more vulnerable in contracting and living with HIV/AIDS."[195] The control of women and girls in eastern Congo over their sex lives is even further weakened in the context of the current war and their vulnerability to contracting HIV/AIDS thus even greater.

The risk of HIV transmission in intercourse that results from sexual violence is, moreover, much higher than during consensual sex. Genital injuries,

---

[192] Human Rights Watch interview, Bukavu, October 16, 2001.

[193] Human Rights Watch interview with Cory Kik, Médecins Sans Frontières - Holland, in Bukavu, October 16, 2001.

[194] UNIFEM, "UNAIDS Partners with UNIFEM to Halt Spread of HIV/AIDS among Women and Girls" (press statement), May 24, 2001.

[195] U.N. Commission on the Status of Women, "Agreed Conclusions on Women, the Girl Child and HIV/AIDS," (statement adopted at the 45th session of the Commission, March 2001).

including tearing and abrasion of the vaginal wall or other organs, increase the likelihood of transmission if the assailant is HIV-positive. In addition, protective vaginal secretions that are normally present in uncoerced sex are absent in cases of rape. Girls who have not yet reached puberty are at particular risk of HIV transmission as they are more likely than older girls and women to suffer genital injuries during rape.[196]

During the 1996-1997 war in the Congo, military authorities distributed condoms to some soldiers, but they then stopped that practice. According to one RCD military doctor, military authorities now treat the subject as taboo and were doing nothing to prevent or limit the spread of the virus in RCD ranks. He noted that the prevalence of HIV/AIDS among RCD troops is "very high," and that it is even higher among the wives and children of these soldiers.[197] He warned that unless the taboo is broken, many more people will die.[198]

The RPA is, however, taking some steps to deal with HIV/AIDS prevention and treatment within its ranks, including opening a testing center at Kanombe military hospital in 2001 and having Population Services International carry out

---

[196] U.S. National Institutes of Health, National Institute of Allergy and Infectious Disease, Fact Sheet: HIV Infection in Women, May 2001. Available at http://www.niaid.nih.gov/factsheets/womenhiv.htm. (accessed May 24, 2002)

[197] The doctor estimated the percentage to be considerably higher than most estimates of the rate for the population at large but he was reluctant to have Human Rights Watch to publish this information. Human Rights Watch telephone interview, Goma, October 26, 2001.

[198] Human Rights Watch telephone interview, Goma, October 26, 2001.

an eighteen-month project focused on preventing HIV/AIDS and distributing condoms to RPA troops.[199]The project, which is funded by the U.S. Agency for International Development, operates only in Rwanda and does not include education on sexual violence.[200] This project obviously faces a large challenge. A recent study reported in a Rwandan newspaper that soldiers' "life expectancy impressions" helped account for the high HIV prevalence among them.[201] It is frequently reported that soldiers and others who feel they stand a high risk of dying anyway do not take precautions against contracting HIV.

---

[199] For instance a Rwandan newspaper reported that Kanombe Military Hospital in Kigali is to open an HIV/AIDS counseling and testing center before the end of 2001 funded by the United States Agency for International Development (USAID). "Army to open testing and counseling centre," *New Times*, November 1-4, 2001, p.5.

[200] Human Rights Watch interview with Amy Power, program manager, Population Services International (Washington, D.C.), January 15, 2002.

[201] "4 percent of RPA are HIV positive - Doctor," *New Times*, November 5-7, 2001, p.4.

INDIVIDUAL AND COMMUNITY RESPONSES

Strategies of Protection

Women and girls of eastern Congo, their families, and the larger community have developed different strategies to protect them from sexual violence. Some families have sent their women and girls to safer locations. A Bukavu resident told Human Rights Watch researchers, "I have a girl in my house whose parents sent her away to keep her from being raped."[202] In other cases, most of the family has fled to safer areas.[203] A priest from a rural parish said, "Women, girls and young men are not in the villages anymore—you only find old people."[204]

Another frequently used strategy is seeking safety in numbers. When possible women and girls try to go to market, to the forest, or to the fields in groups, hoping thus to discourage assailants.[205] Sometimes effective, this practice at other times just delivers larger numbers of women and girls into the hands of assailants. In a variant of this strategy, older women, thought to be less vulnerable to attack, have replaced young women and girls in carrying out activities that require traveling some distance from home. Useful in protecting those who might otherwise be most targeted, this strategy provides no protection for the older women. And as one fourteen-year-old who had been raped commented, "I don't think there is a way to protect ourselves from this. Now we try to make it so the older women go for the charcoal, but at some time everyone will have to go."[206]

In some communities men accompanied groups of women and girls going to market or to cultivate their fields. In one case documented by Human Rights Watch researchers, a man accompanying a group of women tried unsuccessfully to defend one of them when an armed soldier tried to rape her. He was himself shot by the soldier and now suffers from a permanent disability.[207]

In towns some women and girls now wear an extra layer of clothes known as *umugondo* or just *gondo* to make it more difficult for assailants to get at their bodies.[208]

If confronted by armed men who intended to rape them, some women and girls have fought back, using their wits as well as their fists and feet. Some have

---

[202] Human Rights Watch interview, Bukavu, October 16, 2001.

[203] Human Rights Watch group meeting, Goma, October 23, 2001.

[204] Human Rights Watch interview, October 17, 2001.

[205] Human Rights Watch interview, Bukavu, October 15, 2001.

[206] Human Rights Watch interview, Murhesa, October 19, 2001.

[207] Human Rights Watch interview, Goma, October 25, 2001.

[208] Human Rights Watch interview, Goma, October 25, 2001.

tried to shame or persuade their assailants to leave them alone while others have resisted physically or fled. Given the disproportionate power in the hands of the assailants, relatively few women and girls succeeded in escaping rape and other injuries. As a nurse-counselor explained: "Most [perpetrators] say they are going to kill them [the victims]. They say 'how much does it cost to kill you—one bullet, one dollar.' The girls say they then give in."[209]

Response by Civil Society

The scale and horror of sexual violence against women and girls in eastern Congo have prompted churches, human rights associations, women's rights groups and other NGOs to assist the victims and to push for the protection of women's rights.

Churches and some local NGOs provided both material and emotional support to women and girls who had been raped, otherwise sexually abused, or abducted. Some gave material assistance to enable women to resume life in the community after having been abducted for long periods away from home. Some helped victims to resettle in the city, away from villages where they were stigmatized. Often they offered moral support, with church staff or members listening to the victim's story and giving advice.

Churches and local NGOs, not the de facto Rwandan and RCD authorities, deliver medical care to rape victims. In the absence of any functioning official health system, churches and NGOs set up small clinics where raped women are treated for injuries and, in some places, tested for HIV and sexually transmitted diseases. This is being done with minimal funding. In addition, some human rights groups assist victims in seeking treatment for more complicated injuries, by raising funds and putting them in touch with Congolese and international medical organizations.

In some cases, NGOs and individual lawyers provided legal advice and assistance to those few victims who considered making an official complaint.

An increasing number of women's associations and human rights NGOs have begun denouncing abuses against civilians in the context of the current armed conflict, and violence against women and girls in particular. Investigators went regularly into the rural areas of North and South Kivu, speaking to the victims and witnesses, and they have pulled together a substantial amount of information about sexual violence.[210]

---

[209] Human Rights Watch interview, Bukavu, October 16, 2001.

[210] Héritiers de la Justice, "Situation des Droits de l'Homme en République Démocratique du Congo (RDC) cas du Sud-Kivu. Une population désesperée, délassée et prise en otage," Rapport Avril-Décembre 2000 (Report April to December 2000).

In addition, many rights groups are publicly campaigning against attacks on women and girls in this war. On International Women's Day, March 8, 1999, a coalition of women's organizations produced a poster with the title "Enough is enough—when will the war end?" showing a woman and her children being attacked by soldiers. On March 8, 2000, women's groups organized a "Day without Women," during which women stayed away from public life to protest the toll the war has taken on women. On International Women's Day 2001, the women's movement planned a march to protest rights violations, and a local human rights group distributed a leaflet that read:

> Women say NO to sexual violence used as a weapon of war in South Kivu in the Democratic Republic of Congo. The rape of women and girls, without distinction of age, by armed men in our villages must be punished as a crime against humanity. We have never wished nor planned the war in our country, the Democratic Republic of Congo. Why do we have to be the first victims?

RCD authorities, who engaged in regular harassment of human rights activists and others whom they see as representing critical voices of dissent, prohibited activities and marches planned by women's and rights groups and threatened some of the women's leaders.[211] RCD authorities harassed human rights activists, including women's rights leaders, and sometimes imprisoned and beat them. In July 2001 RCD authorities briefly detained a women's rights activist in Goma and in August 2001: they briefly held Gégé Katana, who leads a women's network in Uvira, and her husband Jules Nteba, who heads an NGO for adult education.[212]

Civil society actors have agreed on a program of demands that they are taking to the Inter-Congolese Dialogue, including a recommendation for an international criminal tribunal to judge grave human rights abuses in Congo. This is coupled with a call for a truth and reconciliation commission charged with investigating abuses since 1960, and insistence upon initiating a meaningful process of reconciliation and dialogue in the country.   Other

---

[211] See also chapter on attacks on women's groups in Human Rights Watch, "Eastern Congo Ravaged," p.27-28.

[212] Human Rights Watch press release, "Congolese Activist Detained and Beaten in Eastern Congo" (New York, November 25, 2001) and "Eastern Congo: Rebels' Persecution of Rights Activists" (New York, August 21, 2001). Human Rights Watch interviews, Bujumbura, August, 2001 and Goma and Bukavu, August and October, 2001.

important recommendations concern the withdrawal of foreign troops and democratic reform.[213]

In October 2001, thirty-five human rights activists and women's leaders came together to devise strategies to combat violence against women in the context of the war. Their recommendations built upon the program developed by other civil society organizations, making several more specific recommendations with regards to the protection of women. They demanded, for example, that an international criminal tribunal prosecute sexual crimes and that the U.N. deploy more resources to assist women and girls who are victims of sexual violence and those affected by HIV/AIDS. They also called for legal reform aimed at treating women and men as equals and for legal protection of women affected by HIV/AIDS.[214]

---

[213] Interview with Marie Shimati, women's delegate of civil society for North Kivu, Goma, October 27, 2001. The full program of civil society is presented in: Rapport de la concertation inter-provinciale des forces vives, Bukavu, du 4 au 10 octobre 2001.

[214] Recommendations de l'atelier de formation et de consultation sur les violences contre les femmes en situation de guerre, Goma, 22-23 octobre 2001.

THE RESPONSE OF THE AUTHORITIES

Lack of Protection

The de facto authorities, the RCD and Rwandan forces that support them, have taken few meaningful steps to protect women and girls against rape either by its soldiers or those of its adversaries. According to witnesses, RCD soldiers and Rwandan government backers rarely intervene when civilians are attacked, even in the immediate vicinity of their military posts. They routinely wait until the attack is over and then make reprisal attacks against the enemy or against the civilian population itself which it suspects of disaffection. RCD troops and the Local Defense Force created by the authorities have in some cases helped women escape their captors in forests near Shabunda,[215] but according to witnesses, Local Defense men who accompanied women to the fields for their protection commonly ran away when they were attacked.[216]

When asked how security could be improved, one girl who was raped along with her two younger sisters and two friends replied:

> Maybe they need to send better soldiers to the neighborhoods. We need a better governor and a better government [than the RCD]. With this government, no one has the least pity for anyone. They kill people just like that. We really need peace. You can accept being poor if you can have some peace in your home and in the country. Instead we are attacked.[217]

Justice and Impunity

The RCD retained the pre-war legal code and much of the administrative structure and personnel of the judicial system. As with many state employees, most prosecutorial and judicial personnel were not paid or were paid very irregularly.[218] As the socio-economic situation deteriorated for the vast majority of the population, judicial personnel increasingly relied on bribery and corruption to earn their living. Civilians seeking justice had to pay for the service. And, as one activist told Human Rights Watch, "In court cases today, whoever has the money wins."[219]

---

[215] See pp.44-45.

[216] Human Rights Watch interview, Shabunda, October 22, 2001.

[217] Human Rights Watch interview, Bukavu, October 18, 2001.

[218] In March 2000, Human Rights Watch was told that some had been paid only twice since the current war had begun in August 1998. See Human Rights Watch, "Eastern Congo Ravaged," p.17.

[219] Human Rights Watch interview, Goma, March 17, 2000, in Ibid. p. 17.

People now have little faith in the system. Those who should protect them—the army, the police, and those in positions of power and influence such as judicial personnel—instead often preyed upon them. As those who commit crimes of sexual violence went unpunished, other potential abusers observed the tacit acceptance of such crimes and victims learned there was no point in lodging complaints.

Commenting on the fact that few rape cases go to court and that there is rarely a satisfactory outcome with those that do, a Congolese lawyer said:

> You can't have justice in a context like this. Magistrates are not paid. They can't refuse gifts. It's the same with the security services....Women don't see the point of complaining—even if they say something, what will that change?

He also said that in those cases where women did bring charges, it was very hard to get a conviction for crimes of sexual violence. [220]

When victims or their families did complain to authorities about the crimes that had been committed, authorities sometimes initially responded appropriately but then failed to prosecute the assailants. In the case of the rape and murder of the girl whose breast had been cut off before she was slain, RCD officers came to look at the body; the mother dies not know if they did anything more to punish those guilty. In the case of the five-year-old lured off to be raped, a squad known as the Rapid Intervention Police responded to the parents' complaint. Months later, neither of these investigations had produced any result. When fifteen-year-old Grace C. was abducted for eight days in Goma and lower-ranking officials could not or would not locate her, the head of RCD Intelligence had her back home within two hours. The man who abducted her was detained briefly and then released. The family decided not to pursue the case both for the security of the girl and "to preserve her dignity." They sent her out of the area. [221] A war widow complained about having been raped by a policeman. He was removed and transferred to another post, but he was replaced

---

[220] Human Rights Watch interview, Goma, October 25, 2001.

[221] Electronic communication from family member to Human Rights Watch, December 2001; Human Rights Watch telephone interview, December 2001. The case of Grace has been explained in more detail in the chapter on Sexual Violence against Children and the Elderly.

by another who soon began sexually harassing the woman. She commented, " You can't go anywhere to complain—it's all corruption."[222]

Victims and their families believed they were especially unlikely to get action from the RCD authorities if the perpetrator was part of the RCD or the Rwandan Patriotic Army. A man who had tried to save a woman from rape by a Rwandan army soldier, himself sustaining serious injuries in the process, delivered a gun taken from the rapist to the local administration. But, he said, he expected no further action because the attacker was Rwandan. "It's just that the authorities won't do anything against these Rwandans," he said.[223] A mother who believes her daughter's rapist will escape punishment explained that he had "the power to knock at the door of the Tutsi for help."[224]

Some obstacles to bringing rapists to justice predated the current crisis of war and economic disintegration. Neither the law nor police procedure makes any provision for protecting witnesses and ensuring confidentiality of proceedings. In deciding whether or not to bring charges against suspected perpetrators, victims and their families must consider not only the likelihood of punishing the criminal but also the likelihood of themselves suffering reprisals in the meantime. As one Congolese woman commented, "People are suspected but there is no punishment. If we went and denounced [the perpetrators], they [the authorities] would go and tell them [the accused] and they'd come back and kill you. Someone said your tongue kills you."[225]A Congolese lawyer said that he had advised several rape victims about bringing complaints, but that the women were reluctant to go forward with judicial proceedings because they feared for their safety:

> It is a problem that legal cases are made public. Witness protection is necessary....The structure of the judiciary needs to be reviewed. Unfortunately closed sessions are not foreseen for rape cases.[226]

Under the Family Code, married women do not have full legal rights equal to those of a man; for example they must have their husband's authorization to

---

[222] Human Rights Watch interview, Goma, October 25, 2001.

[223] Human Rights Watch interview, Goma, October 25, 2001.

[224] Human Rights Watch interview, Goma, October 27, 2001. As discussed above, the Tutsi are seen as holding the real power not just in Rwanda but also in eastern Congo.

[225] Human Rights Watch interview, October 19, 2001.

[226] Communication in Goma, October 22, 2001.

initiate judicial action. Preferring to resolve such cases without involving the authorities, male relatives of victims sometimes negotiate a settlement with the perpetrator or his family. For example, sometimes the family of a girl who was raped decides that she should marry her rapist.[227] Local women's associations have documented several cases of the same type and condemned this practice vigorously. Not only is it a fundamental breach of a woman's or girl's right to choose her husband, it also shows how little importance society attaches to violence against women.

In this climate of impunity and violence against the whole population, everyone, including women and the girls subjected to sexual violence, feels powerless to respond to violations. Rape and other forms of sexual violence are increasing and are being committed by an ever-wider range of perpetrators. Women and girls and other members of their communities, from civilians to members of police forces, need to be empowered to resist and respond to such attacks. Implementing the rule of law is a first step towards that empowerment. Ensuring the safety, confidentiality if sought, and treatment with dignity of those who come forward to testify as survivors or as witnesses is an essential step. The message must be clear that rape is unacceptable in society.

Human Rights Watch researchers raised these concerns with the Head of the Department of Justice of the RCD, Moïse Nyarugabo.[228] He acknowledged that sexual violence was a problem in the area but said that no RCD soldiers had been prosecuted because there had been no complaints against them.

A Human Rights Watch researcher met with Col. Andrew Rwigamba, the RPA Military Prosecutor, who said that he had received complaints of RPA soldiers committing crimes of sexual violence in Congo, but that he lacked the necessary evidence to prosecute the cases. He pointed out that the RPA does not have investigators on the ground in Congo to gather the evidence promptly and

---

[227] Human Rights Watch interview, Sake, October 26, 2001. Under Congolese law, a girl must be aged fifteen or over before she is legally allowed to marry (art. 352, Family Code).

[228] Human Rights Watch interview, Goma, October 26, 2001.

said that later investigations were likely to produce inadequate proof to establish guilt.[229]

---

[229] Human Rights Watch interview with Lt. Col. Andrew Rwigamba, Kigali, November 8, 2001.

LEGAL PROTECTION AGAINST SEXUAL VIOLENCE

Congolese Law

The RCD has publicly claimed that it is applying Congolese law. According to international humanitarian law, Congolese laws continue to apply in areas of Congo which are not under the control of the government. National legislation continues in force in an occupied territory and de facto authorities are responsible for maintaining public order and ensuring that courts continue to function for all crimes covered by this legislation. This applies to all armed groups operating on Congolese soil.

The Congolese Penal Code prohibits rape and indecent assault. Rape is defined as forcible sexual penetration, while indecent assault is a sexual assault without penetration. Rape is punishable by a prison sentence of five to twenty years, and indecent assault is punishable by prison terms between six months and twenty years, depending on the age of the victim and whether violence, ruse, or threat were used.[230] Kidnapping or detaining a person using violence, ruse, or threat is also punishable under the Congolese Penal Code. If the victim is subjected to physical torture, the punishment is five to twenty years. If the torture leads to the death of the victim, the death sentence or a life prison sentence are applicable.[231]

The status of women under Congolese law is that of second class citizens.[232] The Family Code defines the husband as the head of the household and determines that his wife has to obey him. Article 444 reads:

"The husband is the head of the household. His duty is the protection of his wife; his wife owes her obedience to her husband."[233]

A woman has to live with her husband wherever he chooses to live.[234] Women must have their husbands' authorization to bring a case in court or to

---

[230] Code pénal, arts. 167, 168, 170, 171.

[231] Code pénal, art. 67. Human Rights Watch is opposed to the death penalty in all circumstances.

[232] Two women's rights associations, Réseau Action Femmes in Kinshasa, and PAIF in Goma, have produced critical comments on the status of women under Congolese law. See Réseau Action Femmes, "Notes from workshop, November 23-24, 2001" and PAIF, "Les articles de la législation zaïroise en contradiction avec les droits de femmes protégés par la convention internationale".

[233] Code zaïrois de la famille, art. 444: "Le mari est le chef du ménage. Il doit protection à sa femme; la femme doit obéissance à son mari." Translation into English by Human Rights Watch.

initiate other legal proceedings. If the husband refuses to allow his wife this authorization, a family council may overrule him, but without such a decision, the wife may not act.[235] The situation of unmarried women is slightly better; the law does not require them to obtain permission from male family members for legal actions.

Certain dispositions of the Congolese Family Code contradict international women's rights as they have been spelt out in the Convention on the Elimination of All Forms of Discrimination against Women (CEDAW) and the International Covenant on Civil and Political Rights (ICCPR), which have both been ratified by the Congolese government. The terms of the Code specifically violate the international standards requiring the equality of men and women before the law, for example, with reference to women's legal capacity, freedom to choose a residence and to dissolve marriage.[236]

International Law

Humanitarian Law

Given the involvement of foreign government troops fighting on Congolese soil, the conflict in Congo has both an international and an internal dimension. Different legal regimes apply to acts committed by different forces in eastern Congo, described in this report.

The legal regime related to international armed conflict in Congo is set out in the Geneva Conventions of 1949 and the First Protocol Additional to the Geneva Conventions of 12 August 1949 relating to the Protection of Victims of International Armed Conflicts (Protocol I). In 1961, Congo ratified the Geneva Conventions, and in 1982, it ratified Protocol I. Rwanda and Burundi, the two foreign powers involved in the conflict in eastern Congo's Kivu provinces, are also state parties to the Geneva Conventions of August 12, 1949 and Protocol

---

[234] Ibid., art. 454: "L'épouse est obligée d'habiter avec son mari et de le suivre partout où il juge à propos de résider; le mari est obligé de la reçevoir." ("The wife has to live with her husband and follow him anywhere he chooses to reside; the husband has to allow her to live with him.").

[235] Ibid., arts. 448-450. In practice, this provision is mostly applied to civil cases; in criminal cases, women often do go to court without permission from their husband. Human Rights Watch telephone interview with Congolese lawyer, February 8, 2002.

[236] Convention on the Elimination of All Forms of Discrimination Against Women, arts. 15 and 16. For further details on the Convention see next chapter.

I.[237] Internal conflict is regulated by Common Article 3 to the Geneva Conventions applicable in situations of armed conflict "not of an international character." Both legal regimes governing the armed conflict in Congo prohibit sexual violence as a severe infraction.

Common Article 3 of the 1949 Geneva Conventions prohibits attacks on those taking no active part in hostilities including civilians. Among the acts prohibited are "(a) Violence to life and person, in particular murder of all kinds, mutilation, cruel treatment and torture; (b) Taking of hostages; (c) Outrages upon personal dignity, in particular humiliating and degrading treatment." Common Article 3 expressly applies to "each party to the conflict," i.e. not only government armies but also armed groups. In eastern Congo, Mai Mai rebels, Rwandan and Burundian Hutu armed groups, as well as the Congolese Rally for Democracy and the Rwandan and Burundian government forces are all bound by the provisions of Common Article 3 which demands "respect for certain rules, which" are, in the words of the commentary to the Geneva Conventions, "already recognized as essential in all civilised countries."

The Fourth Geneva Convention Relative to the Protection of Civilian Persons in Time of War makes specific provisions on sexual violence. Article 27 states that "Women shall be especially protected against any attack on their honor, in particular against rape, enforced prostitution, or any form of indecent assault." This provision is binding for the contracting parties taking part in an international conflict. As the Congolese, Rwandan and Burundian government have all ratified the Geneva Conventions, their troops must abide by this standard.

The First Protocol Additional to the Geneva Conventions of 12 August 1949 relating to the Protection of Victims of International Armed Conflicts (Protocol I) also prohibits acts of sexual violence. Article 76(1) stipulates that "women shall be the object of special respect and shall be protected in particular against rape, forced prostitution and any other form of indecent assault." Protocol I refers to situations of international armed conflict.

International humanitarian law also prohibits acts or threats of violence with the primary purpose of spreading terror among the civilian population, as well as murder, physical or mental torture, rape, mutilation, enforced prostitution, pillage, collective punishments, or the taking of hostages. Methods of warfare

---

[237] Rwanda signed the Geneva Conventions in 1964 and acceded to Protocol I and Protocol II on internal armed conflict in 1984. Burundi signed the Geneva Conventions in 1971 and acceded to Protocol I and Protocol II in 1993.

likely to put the health or survival of the population in danger are also prohibited.[238]

The crime of rape rises to the level of grave breach of the Geneva Conventions (war crime) regardless of whether it occurs on a demonstrably massive scale or is associated with an overarching policy. When rape occurs on a mass scale or as a matter of orchestrated policy, this added dimension of the crime is recognized by designating and prosecuting rape as a crime against humanity.[239] It is only recently that rape and other forms of sexual violence have been prosecuted as war crimes and crimes against humanity. The ad-hoc tribunals of the U.N. have played a key role in this process.

Legal and Political Steps Towards the Recognition of Rape as a War Crime

Despite these legal provisions, rape and other forms of sexual violence have long been dismissed as an unfortunate but common side-effect of war. Sexual violence has been used in many wars as a means to terrify the civilian population, but military and political leaders have shown little willingness to address the issue. This is illustrated by the struggle of the "comfort women," mostly Korean women who were used as sexual slaves by the Japanese army during World War II, to get an official apology from the Japanese government.[240] Sexual violence in wartime is also underreported. As the U.N. special rapporteur on the causes and consequences of violence against women has pointed out: "[Rape] remains the least condemned war crime; throughout history, the rape of hundreds of thousands of women and children in all regions of the world has been a bitter reality."[241]

If these crimes are denounced, they tend to be exposed as uniquely horrific and not understood as the result of a complex set of abuses and discriminatory patterns against women and girls. In other situations, unsubstantiated reports

---

[238] Geneva Convention Relative to the Protection of Civilians in Time of War; Protocol Additional to the Geneva Conventions of 12 August 1949, and relating to the Protection of Victims of International Armed Conflicts (Protocol I), 8 June 1977.

[239] Theodor Meron, "Rape as a Crime under International Humanitarian Law," , American Journal of International Law 87 (1993): 424, 246, 427. See also Dorothy Q. Thomas and Regan E. Ralph, "Rape in War: Challenging the Tradition of Impunity," SAIS Review, Winter-Spring 1994, p.86.

[240] Ibid.

[241] Preliminary Report submitted by the Special Rapporteur on Violence against Women, its Causes and Consequences, Commission on Human Rights, Fiftieth Session, November 1994, U.N. Document E/CN.41995/42, p.64.

about rape have been used to justify military action, for example in the case of Kosovo.[242]

Over the last decade, women's and human rights activists have forced more serious attention to these crimes. As a result important steps have been taken at the international level to prosecute rape and other sexual violence as a war crime.[243] The statutes of the International Criminal Tribunal for the former Yugoslavia and the International Criminal Tribunal for Rwanda (ICTR) explicitly list rape as a crime under their jurisdictions. Both tribunals have indicted and convicted defendants for this war crime. In 1998, the ICTR found Jean-Paul Akayesu, the former mayor of Taba commune in Rwanda, guilty of nine counts of genocide, crimes against humanity, and war crimes. The verdict marked the first time an international court found rape to be an act of genocide. Even this important step toward securing accountability for violence against women came only after a protracted struggle: When Akayesu was first charged in 1996, the twelve counts in his indictment did not include sexual violence.[244] In 2001, the ICTY convicted Bosnian Serbs Dragoljub Kunarac, Radomir Kovac and Zoran Vukovic for rape, torture, and enslavement committed in Foca during the Bosnian war. This case marked the first time in history that an international tribunal brought charges expressly—and only—for crimes of sexual violence against women.[245]

---

[242] Rhonda Copelon, "Gendered War Crimes: Reconceptualizing Rape in Time of War," In *Women's Rights, Human Rights: International Feminist Perspectives*, ed. Julie Peters and Andrea Wolper (New York: Routledge, 1995), pp.197-214. On the manipulation of rape in war, see Human Rights Watch, "Kosovo: Rape as a Weapon of 'Ethnic Cleansing'" *A Human Rights Watch Report,* vol.12, no 3 (D), March 2000, p.8.

[243] See also United Nations, Vienna Declaration and Programme of Action adopted by the World Conference on Human Rights held in Vienna from 14 to 25 June 1993, (A/CONF.157/24), October 13, 1993. art. 38 of the Vienna Declaration and Programme of Action states: "Violations of the human rights of women in situations of armed conflict are violations of the fundamental principles of international human rights and humanitarian law. All violations of this kind, including in particular murder, systematic rape, sexual slavery, and forced pregnancy, require a particularly effective response."

[244] This happened despite the fact that Human Rights Watch and other rights groups had documented widespread rape during the genocide, particularly in the Taba commune. During the Akayesu trial, held intermittently from January 9, 1997 to March 23, 1998, Rwandan women testified that they had been subjected to repeated rapes by militia in and around the Taba commune office, sometimes in view of Akayesu. See *Human Rights Watch World Report 1999*, chapter on women's rights. See also Agnès Callamard, "Investigating Women's Rights Violations in Armed Conflicts," Amnesty International Publications and the International Centre for Human Rights and Democratic Development, 2001, chapter 1 on international justice.

[245] *Human Rights Watch World Report 2002*, chapter on Bosnia and Herzegovina.

Another important step forward is the explicit recognition of sexual violence as part of the mandate of the International Criminal Court. The Rome Statute of the International Criminal Court of 17 July 1998 specifies several types of war crimes and crimes against humanity which are in the competence of the court. These include rape, sexual slavery, enforced prostitution, forced pregnancy, enforced sterilization, or any other form of sexual violence of comparable gravity.[246] Congo ratified the Rome Statute on April 11, 2002.

International Human Rights Law

Many elements of international human rights law relate to sexual violence and to crimes that target women and girls in a discriminatory manner. Article 9 of the International Covenant on Civil and Political Rights (ICCPR), for instance, provides that: "Everyone has the right to liberty and security of person."[247] The ICCPR, like many other human rights instruments, is explicit in affirming "the equal right of men and women to the enjoyment" of all rights it covers.[248] Congo is a party to the ICCPR. The ICCPR as well as the Convention against Torture and Other Cruel Inhuman and Degrading Treatment or Punishment (CAT) prohibit torture under all circumstances. Congo ratified the CAT in 1996. The convention defines torture as "any act by which severe pain or suffering, whether physical or mental, is intentionally inflicted on a person....when such pain or suffering is inflicted by or at the instigation of or with the consent or acquiescence of a public official or other person acting in an official capacity."[249] The Convention on the Elimination of All Forms of Discrimination against Women (CEDAW), to which Congo is also a party, reinforces state responsibility in ensuring "without delay" that any "act or practice of discrimination against women" be stopped.[250]

In a 1993 resolution, the U.N. General Assembly declared that prohibiting gender discrimination includes eliminating gender-based violence and that states "should pursue by all appropriate means and without delay a policy of

---

[246] Rome Statute, art. 7(g).

[247] International Covenant on Civil and Political Rights (ICCPR), art. 9(1).

[248] ICCPR art. 3.

[249] Convention against Torture and Other Cruel Inhuman and Degrading Treatment or Punishment, art. (1).

[250] Convention on the Elimination of All Forms of Discrimination Against Women, art. 2(d).

eliminating violence against women."[251]   The CEDAW Committee enumerated a wide range of obligations of states related to combating sexual violence, including ensuring appropriate treatment for victims in the justice system, counseling and support services, and medical and psychological assistance to victims.[252]

The Convention on the Rights of the Child (CRC) requires states parties to protect children from "all forms of physical or mental violence, injury or abuse, neglect or negligent treatment, maltreatment or exploitation including sexual abuse."[253]   States are also enjoined to provide special protection and assistance to a child "temporarily or permanently deprived of his or her family environment."[254]   Congo is a party to the CRC.   A child's right to "such measures of protection as are required by his status as a minor" is also guaranteed by the ICCPR.[255]

The African Charter on Human and Peoples' Rights, to which Congo is a party, guarantees the "elimination of every discrimination against women...and

---

[251] United Nations General Assembly, "Declaration on the Elimination of Violence against Women," A/RES/48/104, December 20, 1993 (issued on February 23, 1994), esp. art. 4.

[252] Committee on the Elimination of All Forms of Discrimination Against Women, "Violence Against Women," General Recommendation no. 19 (eleventh session, 1992), U.N. Document CEDAW/C/1992/L.1/Add.15.

[253] Convention on the Rights of the Child, art. 19 (1).

[254] Ibid., art. 20 (1).

[255] ICCPR, art. 24 (1).

protection of the rights of the woman and the child"[256] as well as the right to integrity of one's person, the right to be free of "all forms of exploitation and degradation....particularly slavery, slave trade, torture, cruel, inhuman or degrading punishment and treatment."[257]

---

[256] African (Banjul) Charter on Human and Peoples' Rights, adopted June 27, 1981, Organization of African Unity Doc. CAB/LEG/67/3 rev. 5, 21 I.L.M. 58, 1982, art. 3.

[257] African Charter on Human and Peoples' Rights, arts. 4 and 5.

RESPONSE OF THE INTERNATIONAL COMMUNITY

The international response to the catastrophic human rights situation in Congo has been grossly incommensurate with the scale of a problem that has reportedly cost over 2.5 million lives. There have been important efforts towards peace and a rhetorical commitment to accountability, but such initiatives have been undermined by the ongoing violence as well as by contradictory and sometimes misguided policies by donor governments and the United Nations. There have been no effective efforts to address severe human rights violations, including sexual violence against women and girls. The profound impact of such crimes on the victims and their larger communities, combined with the rapidly growing threat of HIV/AIDS in the region, demand a prompt and focused international response.

International actors treat the Lusaka accord as the key to peace in Congo, including its three interlinked elements, 1) disarmament, demobilization, repatriation, resettlement, and reintegration (DDRRR) of armed groups, 2) withdrawal of foreign forces, and 3) the Inter-Congolese Dialogue. The assumption that disarmament has to precede troop withdrawal has led to increased pressure on all parties to disarm rebel groups despite the considerable difficulties associated with this process.

The United States

From the start of the war, the United States has professed a commitment to maintaining the national integrity of the Congo but has at the same time given political backing to Rwanda and Uganda, which both field troops of their regular armies in eastern Congo and so threaten that integrity. In the wake of the 1994 genocide and its failure to respond, the U.S. did not question Rwandan claims that its security required Rwandan troops to make war in Congo against remnants of the genocidal forces. It also gave free hand to the Ugandan government, in part because an alliance with Uganda served its policy interests in the Sudan and the Horn of Africa. Even in the face of mounting evidence that Rwandan and Ugandan troops and their Congolese allies had committed war crimes, the U.S. remained largely silent. From the end of the Clinton administration and the beginning of the Bush administration, the U. S. began pursuing a more critical policy towards Rwanda and Uganda and more openly pressuring them to end abuses. But after the September 11 attacks in the United States, the U.S. government has subordinated other policy considerations, including ending human rights violations, to the "war on terrorism." The U.S. designated the Rwandan Hutu rebel group ALIR a "terrorist organization," a measure which has encouraged the Rwandan government to vigorously reaffirm its intention to remain in Congo until ALIR is defeated.[258]

Ineffective in dealing with the war and its attendant human rights abuses, the U.S. has tried to alleviate some of the resulting misery. During the fiscal year 2001, it spent some $98 million for humanitarian relief, including about $5 million under the Great Lakes Justice Initiative. It is now considering funding a program of humanitarian aid for victims of sexual violence in eastern Congo. In the fiscal year 2001, the U.S. devoted some resources to the problem of HIV/AIDS, spending $3.4 million on a program to train police in Bukavu about preventive measures within the police . In the coming year, the U.S. will expand funding for a program of prevention, control, and improved health services. In January 2002, a team from the U.S. Agency for International Development went to Congo to assess possibilities for expanded assistance on the HIV/AIDS problem.[259]

The European Union

The European Union has proved largely ineffective in influencing developments in Congo because the United Kingdom—generally supported by Germany and the Netherlands—has supported Rwanda and Uganda while France—often together with Belgium—has backed the Congo government.[260] In 2001 Germany and the Netherlands moved towards a more critical policy towards Rwanda, responding to concerns about its continued occupation of eastern Congo and its exploitation of Congolese resources.

In January 2002, the French and British Foreign Ministers made a joint mission to the Great Lakes, meant to promote peace in the region as well as to foster the impression of a unified E.U. policy on the area. In February 2002, Belgium's Foreign Minister made a visit to eastern Congo, during which he

---

[258] Terrorism Exclusion List Designees: December 5, 2001. See website of the U.S. Department of State http://www.state.gov/r/pa/prs/ps/2001/index.cfm?docid=6695. (accessed May 23, 2002). The list names the "Army for the Liberation of Rwanda (ALIR) – AKA: Interahamwe, Former Armed Forces (EX-FAR)." It also lists the Ugandan rebel Allied Democratic Forces (ADF) which are fighting the Ugandan government.

[259] Human Rights Watch telephone interview with Mikaela Meredith, Desk Officer for the Congo, Rwanda, and Burundi, U.S. AID, Washington, D.C., January 24, 2002.

[260] There are considerable differences between the approach of the two relevant ministries, the Foreign and Commonwealth Office, and the Department for International Relations. The All Party Parliamentary Group on the Great Lakes and Genocide Prevention of the House of Commons recently completed a mission to Congo and followed this up with a series of recommendations to the British government.

expressed deep concern about the human rights situation, including violence against women.

In December 2001 the E.U. decided to resume aid to Congo, after considerable debate between Britain, France, and Belgium; the European Development Fund is going to provide $108 million aid to Congo for development projects. In late January 2002, the European Commission adopted a new Global Plan for the Congo worth 32 million euros in humanitarian assistance to focus on health and nutrition/food security as well as relief assistance to the least accessible areas.[261]

The United Nations

The Security Council, Secretary-General, and MONUC

Both Secretary-General Kofi Annan and the Security Council have devoted much attention to ending the Congo war and frequently denounced human rights abuses and the humanitarian crisis spawned by it. They have also repeatedly stressed the importance of protecting women in armed conflict. But the strong language of the resolutions ordinarily lacked any effective mechanisms for implementation.

In October 2000, the Security Council held an Open Session on Women and Armed Conflict in which women's NGOs played an instrumental role. It adopted a resolution calling for documenting the impact of armed conflict on women and the role of women in peace-building. Since then the United Nations Development Fund for Women (UNIFEM) has undertaken a major study on the impact of armed conflict on women in more than ten countries around the world, including the Congo. In September 2001, a team of three women visited the Congo in conjunction with this study.

The council was unable to mobilize the political will to launch a major peace-keeping mission in the Congo. In February 2001 the Security Council decided to deploy 2,300 MONUC troops, about half the number originally foreseen, and with no express mandate for civilian protection. The council extended the mandate for MONUC for a year in mid-June and itself affirmed in Resolution 1355 the importance of accountability. But MONUC is not charged to halt violations of humanitarian law and restricts itself to monitoring the implementation of the Lusaka peace accord.[262] MONUC can act only in accord

---

[261]European Commission, "Aid package for the Democratic Republic of the Congo," January 24, 2002, ref: ECHO02-0005EN.

[262] This is also in contradiction with the Report of the Panel on U.N. Peace Keeping Operations, the so-called Brahimi Report, which suggests that "United Nations

with the local authorities—whether the Congo government or the respective rebel force—which makes independent verification of violations extremely difficult.

Sexual Assault and Peacekeepers

In late December 2001 a Congolese woman reportedly delivered an eleven-year-old girl to a Moroccan soldier of the MONUC Peacekeeping force based in Goma who then assaulted the child sexually. Authorities subsequently arrested the woman but the MONUC soldier continues at his post.[263] The U.N. Department of Peacekeeping Operations has told Human Rights Watch that several internal investigations are currently under way, and has confirmed that the soldier remains in the mission area while these are going on. It has also stressed that the U.N. has a "zero-tolerance policy" regarding assaults by U.N. peacekeepers on women and girls.[264]

The Security Council has stated repeatedly its commitment to include a women's rights component in the work of peacekeeping forces. Although the induction program for U.N. military officers includes training in gender awareness and a gender advisor was recently appointed to MONUC, there does not appear to be any specific training for the peacekeeping force on sexual violence. The recent case of alleged rape by a MONUC soldier illustrates the need for effective programs on women's rights and HIV/AIDS within the peacekeeping force.

U.N. Commission for Human Rights

The U.N. Commission for Human Rights has drawn attention to the grave situation in the Congo, though it has been severely under-funded. Roberto Garretón, the U.N. special rapporteur on the situation of human rights in the Congo until October 2001, issued damning reports on abuses by government and rebels alike. He briefed the Security Council several times on human rights abuses in the Congo and in the speech marking the end of his tenure he too called for accountability for past crimes in Congo. His successor Iulia-

---

peacekeepers — troops or police — who witness violence against civilians should be presumed to be authorized to stop it, within their means, in support of basic United Nations principles," http://www.un.org/peace/reports/peace_operations/ (accessed May 23, 2002).

[263] Human Rights Watch telephone interview with human rights organization in Goma, January 15, 2001; IRIN report, January 11, 2001.

[264] Human Rights Watch telephone interview with staff of U.N. Department of Peacekeeping Operations, January 28, 2001.

Antoanella Motoc from Romania visited the Congo in early 2002. The Field Office of the High Commissioner for Human Rights (HRFOC) effectively monitored human rights conditions in the capital and several other locations around the country, assisted the government in implementing reforms, and supported local rights groups. But the work of this important office is hampered by severe lack of funds and personnel.

International Action on HIV/AIDS

The international response to HIV/AIDS in the form of bilateral and multilateral grants and loans for AIDS programs in Africa falls pitifully short of the effort needed to address the pandemic that has cost the lives of over 22 million young adults. In fact the pace of international donor support in terms of assistance per HIV-infected person actually declined by over 50 percent between 1988 and 1997.[265] This decline mirrored a general and dramatic drop in official development assistance from most bilateral donors to all social sectors (not only health).[266] In an effort to mobilize increased donor support for the fight against HIV/AIDS, United Nations Secretary-General Kofi Annan established a global fund in 2000 through which donor states and private sector donors are being encouraged to channel large grants to combat HIV/AIDS, malaria, and tuberculosis. The secretary-general has set U.S. $7 to $10 billion per year as a target for the fund.[267] At this writing, pledges to the fund total about $1.6 billion. The fund is planning to support countries with well-developed national plans for HIV/AIDS, and as a result Congo is unlikely to be a priority. The U.N. organizations and NGOs doing health work on the ground in eastern Congo are interested in doing more to combat HIV/AIDS, but have very limited resources to deal with a vast array of life-threatening problems.

In July 2000, the Security Council adopted Resolution 1308 which calls on countries to address HIV/AIDS in the context of human security. The resolution targets armed forces and peacekeepers for education, training, and prevention efforts and urges voluntary and confidential HIV/AIDS counseling and testing for all national uniformed forces, especially those deployed internationally. Following adoption of the resolution, the U.N.'s Department of Peacekeeping Operations (DPKO) has begun examining how conflict situations raise the risk

---

[265] Amir Attaran and Jeffrey Sachs, "Defining and refining international donor support for combating the AIDS pandemic," *The Lancet* 357 (2001):57-61.

[266] "Aid to poor countries falls again," *Monday Developments* 16, 12 , July 6, 1998.

[267] Associated Press, "African leaders back less costly AIDS drugs, more spending," April 27, 2001.

of HIV infection.[268] In further recognition of the importance of ensuring preventive measures among peacekeepers, the General Assembly meeting in a special session on HIV/AIDS in June 2001 called for inclusion of HIV/AIDS awareness and training into guidelines for peacekeeping personnel.[269]

The World Bank

In December 2001 the World Bank proposed establishing a Multi-Country Demobilization and Reintegration Program (MDRP) and an associated Regional Multi-Donor Trust Fund (RMDTF) to promote regional peace and stability and to facilitate funding for this program.[270] Preliminary plans for the demobilization phase include voluntary HIV/AIDS screening and counseling and plans for the reconciliation phase include providing information and counseling about HIV/AIDS. At this writing, the plan did not address gender violence or the broader humanitarian and human rights effects of the conflict.

---

[268] UNAIDS press release, "AIDS now core issue at UN Security Council," New York, January 19, 2001.

[269] UNAIDS press release, "UN Security Council welcomes Declaration," New York, June 28, 2001.

[270] The World Bank press release, "Greater Great Lakes Demobilization and Reintegration Program and Trust Fund," Brussels, December 19, 2001.

Rome, 17 July 1998
Entry into force: 1 July 2002, in accordance with article 126.

Article 5
Crimes within the jurisdiction of the Court

1. The jurisdiction of the Court shall be limited to the most serious crimes of concern to the international community as a whole. The Court has jurisdiction in accordance with this Statute with respect to the following crimes:

(a) The crime of genocide;
(b) Crimes against humanity;
(c) War crimes;
(d) The crime of aggression.

2. The Court shall exercise jurisdiction over the crime of aggression once a provision is adopted in accordance with articles 121 and 123 defining the crime and setting out the conditions under which the Court shall exercise jurisdiction with respect to this crime. Such a provision shall be consistent with the relevant provisions of the Charter of the United Nations.

Article 6
Genocide

For the purpose of this Statute, "genocide" means any of the following acts committed with intent to destroy, in whole or in part, a national, ethnical, racial or religious group, as such:

(a) Killing members of the group;
(b) Causing serious bodily or mental harm to members of the group;
(c) Deliberately inflicting on the group conditions of life calculated to bring about its physical destruction in whole or in part;
(d) Imposing measures intended to prevent births within the group;
(e) Forcibly transferring children of the group to another group.

Article 7
Crimes against humanity

1. For the purpose of this Statute, "crime against humanity" means any of the following acts when committed as part of a widespread or systematic attack directed against any civilian population, with knowledge of the attack:

(a) Murder;
(b) Extermination;
(c) Enslavement;
(d) Deportation or forcible transfer of population;
(e) Imprisonment or other severe deprivation of physical liberty in violation of fundamental rules of international law;
(f) Torture;
(g) Rape, sexual slavery, enforced prostitution, forced pregnancy, enforced sterilization, or any other form of sexual violence of comparable gravity;
(h) Persecution against any identifiable group or collectivity on political, racial, national, ethnic, cultural, religious, gender as defined in paragraph 3, or other grounds that are universally recognized as impermissible under international law, in connection with any act referred to in this paragraph or any crime within the jurisdiction of the Court;
(i) Enforced disappearance of persons;
(j) The crime of apartheid;
(k) Other inhumane acts of a similar character intentionally causing great suffering, or serious injury to body or to mental or physical health.

2. For the purpose of paragraph 1:

(a) "Attack directed against any civilian population" means a course of conduct involving the multiple commission of acts referred to in paragraph 1 against any civilian population, pursuant to or in furtherance of a State or organizational policy to commit such attack;
(b) "Extermination" includes the intentional infliction of conditions of life, inter alia the deprivation of access to food and medicine, calculated to bring about the destruction of part of a population;
(c) "Enslavement" means the exercise of any or all of the powers attaching to the right of ownership over a person and includes the exercise of such power in the course of trafficking in persons, in particular women and children;

(d) "Deportation or forcible transfer of population" means forced displacement of the persons concerned by expulsion or other coercive acts from the area in which they are lawfully present, without grounds permitted under international law;

(e) "Torture" means the intentional infliction of severe pain or suffering, whether physical or mental, upon a person in the custody or under the control of the accused; except that torture shall not include pain or suffering arising only from, inherent in or incidental to, lawful sanctions;

(f) "Forced pregnancy" means the unlawful confinement of a woman forcibly made pregnant, with the intent of affecting the ethnic composition of any population or carrying out other grave violations of international law. This definition shall not in any way be interpreted as affecting national laws relating to pregnancy;

(g) "Persecution" means the intentional and severe deprivation of fundamental rights contrary to international law by reason of the identity of the group or collectivity;

(h) "The crime of apartheid" means inhumane acts of a character similar to those referred to in paragraph 1, committed in the context of an institutionalized regime of systematic oppression and domination by one racial group over any other racial group or groups and committed with the intention of maintaining that regime;

(i) "Enforced disappearance of persons" means the arrest, detention or abduction of persons by, or with the authorization, support or acquiescence of, a State or a political organization, followed by a refusal to acknowledge that deprivation of freedom or to give information on the fate or whereabouts of those persons, with the intention of removing them from the protection of the law for a prolonged period of time.

3. For the purpose of this Statute, it is understood that the term "gender" refers to the two sexes, male and female, within the context of society. The term "gender" does not indicate any meaning different from the above.

Article 8
War crimes

1. The Court shall have jurisdiction in respect of war crimes in particular when committed as part of a plan or policy or as part of a large-scale commission of such crimes.

2. For the purpose of this Statute, "war crimes" means:

(a) Grave breaches of the Geneva Conventions of 12 August 1949, namely, any of the following acts against persons or property protected under the provisions of the relevant Geneva Convention:

    i) Willful killing;
    ii) Torture or inhuman treatment, including biological experiments;
    iii) Willfully causing great suffering, or serious injury to body or health;
    iv) Extensive destruction and appropriation of property, not justified by military necessity and carried out unlawfully and wantonly;
    v) Compelling a prisoner of war or other protected person to serve in the forces of a hostile power;
    vi) Willfully depriving a prisoner of war or other protected person of the rights of fair and regular trial;
    vii) Unlawful deportation or transfer or unlawful confinement;
    viii) Taking of hostages.

(b) Other serious violations of the laws and customs applicable in international armed conflict, within the established framework of international law, namely, any of the following acts:

    (i) Intentionally directing attacks against the civilian population as such or against individual civilians not taking direct part in hostilities;
    (ii) Intentionally directing attacks against civilian objects, that is, objects which are not military objectives;
    (iii) Intentionally directing attacks against personnel, installations, material, units or vehicles involved in a humanitarian assistance or peacekeeping mission in accordance with the Charter of the United Nations, as long as they are entitled to the protection given to civilians or civilian objects under the international law of armed conflict;
    (iv) Intentionally launching an attack in the knowledge that such attack will cause incidental loss of life or injury to civilians or damage to civilian objects or widespread, long-term and severe damage to the natural environment which would be clearly excessive in relation to the concrete and direct overall military advantage anticipated;

(v) Attacking or bombarding, by whatever means, towns, villages, dwellings or buildings which are undefended and which are not military objectives;

(vi) Killing or wounding a combatant who, having laid down his arms or having no longer means of defence, has surrendered at discretion;

(vii) Making improper use of a flag of truce, of the flag or of the military insignia and uniform of the enemy or of the United Nations, as well as of the distinctive emblems of the Geneva Conventions, resulting in death or serious personal injury;

(viii) The transfer, directly or indirectly, by the Occupying Power of parts of its own civilian population into the territory it occupies, or the deportation or transfer of all or parts of the population of the occupied territory within or outside this territory;

(ix) Intentionally directing attacks against buildings dedicated to religion, education, art, science or charitable purposes, historic monuments, hospitals and places where the sick and wounded are collected, provided they are not military objectives;

(x) Subjecting persons who are in the power of an adverse party to physical mutilation or to medical or scientific experiments of any kind which are neither justified by the medical, dental or hospital treatment of the person concerned nor carried out in his or her interest, and which cause death to or seriously endanger the health of such person or persons;

(xi) Killing or wounding treacherously individuals belonging to the hostile nation or army;

(xii) Declaring that no quarter will be given;

(xiii) Destroying or seizing the enemy's property unless such destruction or seizure be imperatively demanded by the necessities of war;

(xiv) Declaring abolished, suspended or inadmissible in a court of law the rights and actions of the nationals of the hostile party;

(xv) Compelling the nationals of the hostile party to take part in the operations of war directed against their own country, even if they were in the belligerent's service before the commencement of the war;

(xvi) Pillaging a town or place, even when taken by assault;

(xvii) Employing poison or poisoned weapons;

(xviii) Employing asphyxiating, poisonous or other gases, and all analogous liquids, materials or devices;

(xix) Employing bullets which expand or flatten easily in the human body, such as bullets with a hard envelope which does not entirely cover the core or is pierced with incisions;

(xx) Employing weapons, projectiles and material and methods of warfare which are of a nature to cause superfluous injury or unnecessary suffering or which are inherently indiscriminate in violation of the international law of armed conflict, provided that such weapons, projectiles and material and methods of warfare are the subject of a comprehensive prohibition and are included in an annex to this Statute, by an amendment in accordance with the relevant provisions set forth in articles 121 and 123;

(xxi) Committing outrages upon personal dignity, in particular humiliating and degrading treatment;

(xxii) Committing rape, sexual slavery, enforced prostitution, forced pregnancy, as defined in article 7, paragraph 2 (f), enforced sterilization, or any other form of sexual violence also constituting a grave breach of the Geneva Conventions;

(xxiii) Utilizing the presence of a civilian or other protected person to render certain points, areas or military forces immune from military operations;

(xxiv) Intentionally directing attacks against buildings, material, medical units and transport, and personnel using the distinctive emblems of the Geneva Conventions in conformity with international law;

(xxv) Intentionally using starvation of civilians as a method of warfare by depriving them of objects indispensable to their survival, including willfully impeding relief supplies as provided for under the Geneva Conventions;

(xxvi) Conscripting or enlisting children under the age of fifteen years into the national armed forces or using them to participate actively in hostilities.

(c) In the case of an armed conflict not of an international character, serious violations of article 3 common to the four Geneva Conventions of 12 August 1949, namely, any of the following acts committed against persons taking no active part in the hostilities, including members of armed forces who have laid down their arms and those placed hors de combat by sickness, wounds, detention or any other cause:

(i) Violence to life and person, in particular murder of all kinds, mutilation, cruel treatment and torture;

(ii) Committing outrages upon personal dignity, in particular humiliating and degrading treatment;

(iii) Taking of hostages;

(iv) The passing of sentences and the carrying out of executions without previous judgement pronounced by a regularly constituted court, affording all judicial guarantees which are generally recognized as indispensable.

(d) Paragraph 2 (c) applies to armed conflicts not of an international character and thus does not apply to situations of internal disturbances and tensions, such as riots, isolated and sporadic acts of violence or other acts of a similar nature.

(e) Other serious violations of the laws and customs applicable in armed conflicts not of an international character, within the established framework of international law, namely, any of the following acts:

(i) Intentionally directing attacks against the civilian population as such or against individual civilians not taking direct part in hostilities;

(ii) Intentionally directing attacks against buildings, material, medical units and transport, and personnel using the distinctive emblems of the Geneva Conventions in conformity with international law;

(iii) Intentionally directing attacks against personnel, installations, material, units or vehicles involved in a humanitarian assistance or peacekeeping mission in accordance with the Charter of the United Nations, as long as they are entitled to the protection given to civilians or civilian objects under the international law of armed conflict;

(iv) Intentionally directing attacks against buildings dedicated to religion, education, art, science or charitable purposes, historic monuments, hospitals and places where the sick and wounded are collected, provided they are not military objectives;

(v) Pillaging a town or place, even when taken by assault;

(vi) Committing rape, sexual slavery, enforced prostitution, forced pregnancy, as defined in article 7, paragraph 2 (f), enforced sterilization, and any other form of sexual violence also constituting a serious violation of article 3 common to the four Geneva Conventions;

(vii) Conscripting or enlisting children under the age of fifteen years into armed forces or groups or using them to participate actively in hostilities;

(viii)   Ordering the displacement of the civilian population for reasons related to the conflict, unless the security of the civilians involved or imperative military reasons so demand;

(ix) Killing or wounding treacherously a combatant adversary;

(x) Declaring that no quarter will be given;

(xi) Subjecting persons who are in the power of another party to the conflict to physical mutilation or to medical or scientific experiments of any kind which are neither justified by the medical, dental or hospital treatment of the person concerned nor carried out in his or her interest, and which cause death to or seriously endanger the health of such person or persons;

(xii) Destroying or seizing the property of an adversary unless such destruction or seizure be imperatively demanded by the necessities of the conflict;

(f) Paragraph 2 (e) applies to armed conflicts not of an international character and thus does not apply to situations of internal disturbances and tensions, such as riots, isolated and sporadic acts of violence or other acts of a similar nature. It applies to armed conflicts that take place in the territory of a State when there is protracted armed conflict between governmental authorities and organized armed groups or between such groups.

3. Nothing in paragraph 2 (c) and (e) shall affect the responsibility of a Government to maintain or re-establish law and order in the State or to defend the unity and territorial integrity of the State, by all legitimate means.

THE CONVENTION ON THE ELIMINATION OF ALL FORMS
OF DISCRIMINATION AGAINST WOMEN

Adopted and opened for signature, ratification and accession by General Assembly resolution 34/180 of 18 December 1979; entry into force 3 September 1981, in accordance with article 27(1).

The States Parties to the present Convention,

Noting that the Charter of the United Nations reaffirms faith in fundamental human rights, in the dignity and worth of the human person and in the equal rights of men and women,

Noting that the Universal Declaration of Human Rights affirms the principle of the inadmissibility of discrimination and proclaims that all human beings are born free and equal in dignity and rights and that everyone is entitled to all the rights and freedoms set forth therein, without distinction of any kind, including distinction based on sex,

Noting that the States Parties to the International Covenants on Human Rights have the obligation to ensure the equal rights of men and women to enjoy all economic, social, cultural, civil and political rights,

Considering the international conventions concluded under the auspices of the United Nations and the specialized agencies promoting equality of rights of men and women,

Noting also the resolutions, declarations and recommendations adopted by the United Nations and the specialized agencies promoting equality of rights of men and women,

Concerned, however, that despite these various instruments extensive discrimination against women continues to exist,

Recalling that discrimination against women violates the principles of equality of rights and respect for human dignity, is an obstacle to the participation of women, on equal terms with men, in the political, social, economic and cultural life of their countries, hampers the growth of the prosperity of society and the family and makes more difficult the full development of the potentialities of women in the service of their countries and of humanity,

Concerned that in situations of poverty women have the least access to food, health, education, training and opportunities for employment and other needs,

Convinced that the establishment of the new international economic order based on equity and justice will contribute significantly towards the promotion of equality between men and women,

Emphasizing that the eradication of apartheid, all forms of racism, racial discrimination, colonialism, neo-colonialism, aggression, foreign occupation and domination and interference in the internal affairs of States is essential to the full enjoyment of the rights of men and women,

Affirming that the strengthening of international peace and security, the relaxation of international tension, mutual co-operation among all States irrespective of their social and economic systems, general and complete disarmament, in particular nuclear disarmament under strict and effective international control, the affirmation of the principles of justice, equality and mutual benefit in relations among countries and the realization of the right of peoples under alien and colonial domination and foreign occupation to self-determination and independence, as well as respect for national sovereignty and territorial integrity, will promote social progress and development and as a consequence will contribute to the attainment of full equality between men and women,

Convinced that the full and complete development of a country, the welfare of the world and the cause of peace require the maximum participation of women on equal terms with men in all fields,

Bearing in mind the great contribution of women to the welfare of the family and to the development of society, so far not fully recognized, the social significance of maternity and the role of both parents in the family and in the upbringing of children, and aware that the role of women in procreation should not be a basis for discrimination but that the upbringing of children requires a sharing of responsibility between men and women and society as a whole,

Aware that a change in the traditional role of men as well as the role of women in society and in the family is needed to achieve full equality between men and women,

Determined to implement the principles set forth in the Declaration on the Elimination of Discrimination against Women and, for that purpose, to adopt the measures required for the elimination of such discrimination in all its forms and manifestations,

Have agreed on the following:

PART I

Article I

For the purposes of the present Convention, the term "discrimination against women" shall mean any distinction, exclusion or restriction made on the basis of sex which has the effect or purpose of impairing or nullifying the recognition, enjoyment or exercise by women, irrespective of their marital status, on a basis of equality of men and women, of human rights and fundamental freedoms in the political, economic, social, cultural, civil or any other field.

Article 2
States Parties condemn discrimination against women in all its forms, agree to pursue by all appropriate means and without delay a policy of eliminating discrimination against women and, to this end, undertake:

(a) To embody the principle of the equality of men and women in their national constitutions or other appropriate legislation if not yet incorporated therein and to ensure, through law and other appropriate means, the practical realization of this principle;

(b) To adopt appropriate legislative and other measures, including sanctions where appropriate, prohibiting all discrimination against women;

(c) To establish legal protection of the rights of women on an equal basis with men and to ensure through competent national tribunals and other public institutions the effective protection of women against any act of discrimination;

(d) To refrain from engaging in any act or practice of discrimination against women and to ensure that public authorities and institutions shall act in conformity with this obligation;

(e) To take all appropriate measures to eliminate discrimination against women by any person, organization or enterprise;

(f) To take all appropriate measures, including legislation, to modify or abolish existing laws, regulations, customs and practices which constitute discrimination against women;

(g) To repeal all national penal provisions which constitute discrimination against women.

Article 3
States Parties shall take in all fields, in particular in the political, social, economic and cultural fields, all appropriate measures, including legislation, to en sure the full development and advancement of women, for the purpose of guaranteeing them the exercise and enjoyment of human rights and fundamental freedoms on a basis of equality with men.

Article 4
1. Adoption by States Parties of temporary special measures aimed at accelerating de facto equality between men and women shall not be considered

discrimination as defined in the present Convention, but shall in no way entail as a consequence the maintenance of unequal or separate standards; these measures shall be discontinued when the objectives of equality of opportunity and treatment have been achieved.

2. Adoption by States Parties of special measures, including those measures contained in the present Convention, aimed at protecting maternity shall not be considered discriminatory.

Article 5

States Parties shall take all appropriate measures:

(a) To modify the social and cultural patterns of conduct of men and women, with a view to achieving the elimination of prejudices and customary and all other practices which are based on the idea of the inferiority or the superiority of either of the sexes or on stereotyped roles for men and women;

(b) To ensure that family education includes a proper understanding of maternity as a social function and the recognition of the common responsibility of men and women in the upbringing and development of their children, it being understood that the interest of the children is the primordial consideration in all cases.

Article 6

States Parties shall take all appropriate measures, including legislation, to suppress all forms of traffic in women and exploitation of prostitution of women.

PART II

Article 7

States Parties shall take all appropriate measures to eliminate discrimination against women in the political and public life of the country and, in particular, shall ensure to women, on equal terms with men, the right:

(a) To vote in all elections and public referenda and to be eligible for election to all publicly elected bodies;

(b) To participate in the formulation of government policy and the implementation thereof and to hold public office and perform all public functions at all levels of government;

(b) To participate in non-governmental organizations and associations concerned with the public and political life of the country.

Article 8

States Parties shall take all appropriate measures to ensure to women, on equal terms with men and without any discrimination, the opportunity to represent their Governments at the international level and to participate in the work of international organizations.

Article 9

1. States Parties shall grant women equal rights with men to acquire, change or retain their nationality. They shall ensure in particular that neither marriage to an alien nor change of nationality by the husband during marriage shall automatically change the nationality of the wife, render her stateless or force upon her the nationality of the husband.

2. States Parties shall grant women equal rights with men with respect to the nationality of their children.

PART III

Article 10

States Parties shall take all appropriate measures to eliminate discrimination against women in order to ensure to them equal rights with men in the field of education and in particular to ensure, on a basis of equality of men and women:

(a) The same conditions for career and vocational guidance, for access to studies and for the achievement of diplomas in educational establishments of all categories in rural as well as in urban areas; this equality shall be ensured in pre-school, general, technical, professional and higher technical education, as well as in all types of vocational training;

(b) Access to the same curricula, the same examinations, teaching staff with qualifications of the same standard and school premises and equipment of the same quality;

(c) The elimination of any stereotyped concept of the roles of men and women at all levels and in all forms of education by encouraging coeducation and other types of education which will help to achieve this aim and, in particular, by the revision of textbooks and school programmes and the adaptation of teaching methods;

(d) The same opportunities to benefit from scholarships and other study grants;

(e) The same opportunities for access to programmes of continuing education, including adult and functional literacy programmes, particularly those aimed at reducing, at the earliest possible time, any gap in education existing between men and women;

(f) The reduction of female student drop-out rates and the organization of programmes for girls and women who have left school prematurely;

(g) The same Opportunities to participate actively in sports and physical education;

(h) Access to specific educational information to help to ensure the health and well-being of families, including information and advice on family planning.

Article 11

1. States Parties shall take all appropriate measures to eliminate discrimination against women in the field of employment in order to ensure, on a basis of equality of men and women, the same rights, in particular:

(a) The right to work as an inalienable right of all human beings;

(b) The right to the same employment opportunities, including the application of the same criteria for selection in matters of employment;

(c) The right to free choice of profession and employment, the right to promotion, job security and all benefits and conditions of service and the right to receive vocational training and retraining, including apprenticeships, advanced vocational training and recurrent training;

(d) The right to equal remuneration, including benefits, and to equal treatment in respect of work of equal value, as well as equality of treatment in the evaluation of the quality of work;

(e) The right to social security, particularly in cases of retirement, unemployment, sickness, invalidity and old age and other incapacity to work, as well as the right to paid leave;

(f) The right to protection of health and to safety in working conditions, including the safeguarding of the function of reproduction.

2. In order to prevent discrimination against women on the grounds of marriage or maternity and to ensure their effective right to work, States Parties shall take appropriate measures:

(a) To prohibit, subject to the imposition of sanctions, dismissal on the grounds of pregnancy or of maternity leave and discrimination in dismissals on the basis of marital status;

(b) To introduce maternity leave with pay or with comparable social benefits without loss of former employment, seniority or social allowances;

(c) To encourage the provision of the necessary supporting social services to enable parents to combine family obligations with work responsibilities and participation in public life, in particular through promoting the establishment and development of a network of child-care facilities;

(d) To provide special protection to women during pregnancy in types of work proved to be harmful to them.

3. Protective legislation relating to matters covered in this article shall be reviewed periodically in the light of scientific and technological knowledge and shall be revised, repealed or extended as necessary.

Article 12

1. States Parties shall take all appropriate measures to eliminate discrimination against women in the field of health care in order to ensure, on a basis of equality of men and women, access to health care services, including those related to family planning.

2. Notwithstanding the provisions of paragraph I of this article, States Parties shall ensure to women appropriate services in connection with pregnancy, confinement and the post-natal period, granting free services where necessary, as well as adequate nutrition during pregnancy and lactation.

Article 13

States Parties shall take all appropriate measures to eliminate discrimination against women in other areas of economic and social life in order to ensure, on a basis of equality of men and women, the same rights, in particular:

(a) The right to family benefits;

(b) The right to bank loans, mortgages and other forms of financial credit;

(c) The right to participate in recreational activities, sports and all aspects of cultural life.

Article 14

1. States Parties shall take into account the particular problems faced by rural women and the significant roles which rural women play in the economic survival of their families, including their work in the non-monetized sectors of the economy, and shall take all appropriate measures to ensure the application of the provisions of the present Convention to women in rural areas.

2. States Parties shall take all appropriate measures to eliminate discrimination against women in rural areas in order to ensure, on a basis of equality of men and women, that they participate in and benefit from rural development and, in particular, shall ensure to such women the right:

(a) To participate in the elaboration and implementation of development planning at all levels;

(b) To have access to adequate health care facilities, including information, counseling and services in family planning;

(c) To benefit directly from social security programmes;

(d) To obtain all types of training and education, formal and non-formal, including that relating to functional literacy, as well as, inter alia, the benefit of all community and extension services, in order to increase their technical proficiency;

(e) To organize self-help groups and co-operatives in order to obtain equal access to economic opportunities through employment or self employment;

(f) To participate in all community activities;

(g) To have access to agricultural credit and loans, marketing facilities, appropriate technology and equal treatment in land and agrarian reform as well as in land resettlement schemes;

(h) To enjoy adequate living conditions, particularly in relation to housing, sanitation, electricity and water supply, transport and communications.

PART IV

Article 15

1. States Parties shall accord to women equality with men before the law.

2. States Parties shall accord to women, in civil matters, a legal capacity identical to that of men and the same opportunities to exercise that capacity. In particular, they shall give women equal rights to conclude contracts and to administer property and shall treat them equally in all stages of procedure in courts and tribunals.

3. States Parties agree that all contracts and all other private instruments of any kind with a legal effect which is directed at restricting the legal capacity of women shall be deemed null and void.

4. States Parties shall accord to men and women the same rights with regard to the law relating to the movement of persons and the freedom to choose their residence and domicile.

Article 16

1. States Parties shall take all appropriate measures to eliminate discrimination against women in all matters relating to marriage and family relations and in particular shall ensure, on a basis of equality of men and women:

(a) The same right to enter into marriage;

(b) The same right freely to choose a spouse and to enter into marriage only with their free and full consent;

(c) The same rights and responsibilities during marriage and at its dissolution;

(d) The same rights and responsibilities as parents, irrespective of their marital status, in matters relating to their children; in all cases the interests of the children shall be paramount;

(e) The same rights to decide freely and responsibly on the number and spacing of their children and to have access to the information, education and means to enable them to exercise these rights;

(f) The same rights and responsibilities with regard to guardianship, wardship, trusteeship and adoption of children, or similar institutions where these concepts exist in national legislation; in all cases the interests of the children shall be paramount;

(g) The same personal rights as husband and wife, including the right to choose a family name, a profession and an occupation;

(h) The same rights for both spouses in respect of the ownership, acquisition, management, administration, enjoyment and disposition of property, whether free of charge or for a valuable consideration.

2. The betrothal and the marriage of a child shall have no legal effect, and all necessary action, including legislation, shall be taken to specify a minimum age for marriage and to make the registration of marriages in an official registry compulsory.

PART V
Article 17

1. For the purpose of considering the progress made in the implementation of the present Convention, there shall be established a Committee on the Elimination of Discrimination against Women (hereinafter referred to as the Committee) consisting, at the time of entry into force of the Convention, of eighteen and, after ratification of or accession to the Convention by the thirty-fifth State Party, of twenty-three experts of high moral standing and competence in the field covered by the Convention. The experts shall be elected by States Parties from among their nationals and shall serve in their personal capacity, consideration being given to equitable geographical distribution and to the representation of the different forms of civilization as well as the principal legal systems.